SOCIAL
STUDIES
SOURCES

Erling M. Hunt, Series Editor

Congress and the President:
Readings in Executive-Legislative Relations
By Walter Earl Travis

A Bibliography for Teachers of Social Studies
by Raymond A. Ducharme, Jr., Joseph Katz, and
Arthur D. Sheekey

Honors Teaching in American History
By Lawrence A. Fink (*Fall, 1968*)

An Interpretations Approach in High School American History
by David F. Kellum (*Fall, 1968*)

Charles A. Beard and the Social Studies: A Book of Readings
by Raymond A. Ducharme, Jr. (*Spring, 1969*)

JOHN JAY

Founder of a State and Nation

DONALD L. SMITH

Social Studies Sources
Erling M. Hunt, Series Editor

TEACHERS COLLEGE PRESS
Teachers College, Columbia University
New York, New York

To Derek, Sheryl, and Dana
May always they love the past and seek the truth!

Preface

John Jay was one of the most respected and influential early citizens of his state and nation, yet relatively little has been written that describes his role in shaping the forces that created these political entities. Although the present study contributes no new knowledge of Jay or of the developments in which he was involved, it is intended to add to available resources for the study and teaching of the history of the United States and the State of New York from 1774 through 1789.

Advanced high school and college students need more opportunities to examine source material in order to gain greater "feel" for the personalities and events of history. Too often they are limited by the inadequate resources of their schools or the practical difficulties of time in locating and examining multiple sources, which are essential in the development of important historical insights.

By presenting selections from the writings of John Jay and, occasionally, of his contemporaries, this study organizes a collection of readings that illuminate some of the major political and diplomatic issues of the period 1774–1789, material that clearly reflects Jay's principles or political position in relation to those issues. This collection should enable a student to achieve a greater understanding of the contributions of a self-effacing American to the successful struggle for independence, the creation of the State of New York, and the establishment of a strong constitutional government for the United States.

I am deeply indebted to Erling Hunt for many things, but particularly his timeless efforts in helping to prepare this manuscript. I owe much to three very dear people, Eleanor Smith, and Dorothy and Jack Adams, whose faith and encouragement were constant. Finally I am especially grateful to June Smith for without her help and assistance this study would not have been possible.

New York, New York
August, 1968

DONALD LEWIS SMITH

Foreword

The years during which the thirteen colonies established their independence and a new federal union were crowded with events that textbooks summarize swiftly but often lack space to discuss. The brief outlines cannot explore the complicated problems that threatened the life of the new nation and sharply divided its states and leaders.

Why did many well-to-do subjects of the King organize to oppose British policies and move the Continental Congresses from protest to a declaraion of independence? How did the colonies establish new state governments? What was the policy in the new states for dealing with people who remained British Loyalists? How did the new nation gain support in Europe for a war that it could not win without the aid of powerful allies? How did American diplomats manage to gain a favorable settlement in the Treaty of 1783 and later obtain commercial rights and satisfactory boundary settlements from reluctant European nations? How did supporters of the strong federal union provided by the new Constitution overcome the opposition of the many anti-federalists? How did the new federal government and the several states put the Constitution into operation and make it succeed?

Textbooks allude to such questions, but they fail to go into the detail necessary to understand the problems and the difficulties of the founders of the United States. John Jay, quiet, able, and conscientious, but rarely dramatic, was deeply involved in nonmilitary American affairs, from the early 1770's to the end of the century. His writings lend reality to the critical issues of the period. Dr. Donald Smith's selections from the published papers of John Jay — still incomplete pending the forthcoming volumes edited by Professor Richard B. Morris — plunge readers into troubles, dangers, and frustrations of our early national history. They also illuminate the character and activities of many of Jay's colleagues in founding the State of New York and the United States. The selections make clear the importance of the untiring and solid accomplishment of a major American who was for a long time inadequately recognized in American history — Jay himself.

Erling M. Hunt

Contents

Contents

Contents

CHAPTER I

John Jay in American History and Historiography

John Jay's public career began in 1774, when tensions between the British government and the thirteen colonies were dividing the loyalties of Americans.* It ended when he retired from the governorship of New York in 1801. Somewhat younger than George Washington, John Adams, and Thomas Jefferson, whose careers exceeded his in length and in fame, Jay's activities paralleled theirs in the struggle for independence, the transformation of an English colony into a sovereign state, the development of a transitional confederation of the states, and the establishment of a viable federal union.

Jay in American History

John Jay was born in New York City on December 12, 1745, the son of Peter and Mary Jay, and grandson of Augustus Jay, a prominent French Huguenot forced into exile by the Edict of Nantes, who never let his family forget the strong Calvinistic principles that caused him to emigrate to America. Young John grew up on a reading diet of religious tracts that helped to create within him a deep suspicion of any threat to religious freedom, an intense aversion to the forces that interfered with personal liberty — including the institution of slavery — and a strong, unshakable faith in Divine Providence that permeated his writings and influenced his actions for the rest of his life.

*The most complete account of Jay's life can be found in the biography by Frank Monaghan, *John Jay, Defender of Liberty* (New York: The Bobbs-Merrill Company, edited by Allen Johnson and Dumas Malone (New York: Charles Scribner's Sons, 1935); a valuable shorter account appears in the *Dictionary of American Biography*, 1928–1944. 22 volumes), X, 5–10; a brief summary of the *DAB* sketch, which still provides the essential facts, appears in the *Concise Dictionary of American Biography*, edited by Joseph G. E. Hopkins, *et al.* (New York: Charles Scribner's Sons, 1964), 491–492.

1

A serious young man, John entered King's College, now Columbia University, before he was fifteen. At first he considered the ministry, but he settled on preparing for a career in law. Although his record at college was apparently satisfactory, it included his temporary suspension for refusing to reveal to the president the name of a fellow student who broke up a table in one of the college halls. He was reinstated, however, and graduated with his class in 1764. As New York lawyers had agreed not to take any more law clerks — in an effort to avoid an overgrowth of the profession — Jay was planning to apprentice in England; however, the lawyers modified their agreement, and John was able to prepare for the bar in the office of Benjamin Kissim of New York.

The duties of a law clerk were hard, the hours long, requiring laborious hand copying of legal documents, yet John was dedicated to his work, spending much of his free time on his law books, and he was duly admitted to the bar in 1768. Appointed as a clerk to the commission that was trying to settle disputed boundaries beween New York and New Jersey, Jay witnessed the use of arbitration to resolve the matter, an experience that may well have initiated his interest in arbitration and influenced him to include it as a prominent feature of the treaty he negotiated with England in 1794.

Jay was one of the founders of the Moot, a club of prominent New York lawyers who met once a month to examine and debate points of law. This group brought together Gouverneur Morris and Robert R. Livingston, as well as others who played a vital role in the history of the state, and their discussions may have influenced several decisions of the Supreme Court of New York. Jay immersed himself in his law cases, while at the same time managing to maintain an active social life, including membership in the Social Club of New York. Despite bouts with ill-health, which plagued him all his life, he disposed of over three hundred cases in less than four years, an unusual feat that strengthened both his finances and his reputation.

But the careful, diligent, and successful young lawyer was ready to settle down. William Livingston, first president of the Moot and later revolutionary governor of New Jersey, invited Jay to his home, where he met and fell in love with his host's youngest daughter, Sarah Van Brugh Livingston, called Sally. The two were married in April of 1774. Their relationship was extremely close throughout their marriage. Ten years older than Sally, Jay was worshipped by her, and he in turn adored his wife. His main regret in a career of twenty-seven years in public service seemed to be the lack of available time to spend with her; the value he placed on her companionship was probably an important factor in his remarkable lack of political ambition.

At first Jay remained aloof from provincial politics. The passage of the

2

Stamp Act in 1765 had galvanized the dissident groups of New York into common opposition to the measure, but it also created an air of turbulence that did not clear when the Stamp Act was repealed. Jay's law cases and approaching marriage concerned him more than the unrest, however, and he was looking forward to a secure legal career and a happy domestic life when the Boston Tea Party, and the resulting series of Coercive Acts against the citizens of Massachusetts, projected him into the politics of New York.

He began his political career as a committee member chosen for his conservative views to counterbalance the increasing radical sentiment, and was elected to represent his colony in both the First and the Second Continental Congresses. There he slowly evolved from an inconspicuous conservative to a well-known, highly respected moderate who firmly supported the Patriot cause and from whose pen came the resolution that ratified the Declaration of Independence in New York, binding her to her sister colonies. He became a vital member of the New York system of local colonial government — both in its legislature and its extra-legal committee system — and was the major contributor to the constitution that established the former colony as a state. He was elected the first Chief Justice of New York, and in that capacity he raised the voice of reason, demanding from his fellow patriots *justice* as well as liberty.

Upon his return to the Second Continental Congress, he was elected its president, and in the midst of confusion and intrigue managed to win the respect of most of his fellow delegates. Chosen as Minister Plenipotentiary to Spain, he embarked on surely one of the most frustrating diplomatic assignments of all time. He was never formally received in his official capacity by the Spanish, who were playing the European diplomatic game of dealing with both sides. Despite the public humiliation that he suffered, Jay never forgot that as a representative of a fledgling republic, fighting a precarious struggle for its survival, he must not endanger his country's cause. Even in the face of personal difficulties — his own poor health, his wife's illness, the death of a new-born daughter, and duplicity in his own household that undermined his mission — he remained resolute.

Together with Benjamin Franklin and John Adams, Jay was elected Peace Commissioner albeit with severely limited powers. He transferred from Spain to Paris, where he deliberately violated the terms of the congressional commission in order to help win a treaty of peace that obtained independence and amazingly favorable terms for his country. Returning to the United States, he was appointed Secretary for Foreign Affairs, and gave that office an identity apart from Congress. Even though previously he had been cognizant of the difficulties of the confederation, his new post made him more agonizingly aware of the new nation's limitations in foreign affairs. Despite the frustrations of governmental inefficacy, he maintained the responsibilities of his office, and that our relations with England, Spain, France, and the Barbary States — all presenting major problems — did not deteriorate beyond repair was largely due to Jay's judicious efforts.

His duties in Congress, in Spain and France, and in the Office of Foreign Affairs caused him to react against the concept of limited national power, and he early established himself as a strong advocate of governmental reform. However, while he believed in strong central authority, he regarded the people as the ultimate source of power. Despite his eminence in the state, the New York legislature, fearful of his national views, refused to appoint him to the Philadelphia Convention in 1787. Nevertheless, the instrument of government created by that body clearly reflected Jay's belief in a central authority that was strong enough to exercise power, but also was provided with a system of checks and balances on that power through its separation into legislative, executive, and judicial branches.

In support of the Constitution, Jay, with Hamilton and Madison, wrote *The Federalist,* one of the great documents on political theory in human history. Jay himself drafted only five of the individual essays, yet this relatively small number is hardly indicative of his actual contribution. Of the *first* five documents of the *Federalist,* Jay wrote four, ceasing only when a severe illness prevented further writing for many months. When he was sufficently recovered, he wrote a strong defense of the treaty-making powers of the Senate, which became Number 64 in the series, but Hamilton and Madison had successfully absorbed the slack resulting from Jay's absence, so Jay was able to turn his energies to his own work, *An Address to the People of the State of New York.* Published anonymously, its practical language and moderate tone enabled it to affect people who found the *Federalist* too theoretical, and of the Constitutional documents the *Address* must rank near the *Federalist* in the extent of its influence.

Elected to the Poughkeepsie Convention, which was overwhelmingly against the Constitution, Jay was less spectacular than Hamilton in his efforts to secure New York's adoption of the new government, but his efforts were clearly important. He sensed the divisions in the opposition forces, and by his moderate approach he created a vital bridge linking the less extreme men in both camps. When ratification in New Hampshire and Virginia gave the advocates of the Constitution a clear advantage for the first time, opponents could cross that bridge without loss of face. The writing of the circular letter to the other states — requesting another convention for the purpose of amending the Constitution — was entrusted to Jay, and its tone of conciliation made such a strong appeal to both sides at Poughkeepsie that it was unanimously accepted, setting the stage for the final vote on New York's ratification, which resulted in a narrow victory for the Constitution.

Establishing the new government was a formidable task that demanded that Washington leave retirement at Mount Vernon to serve as President. Among the men Washington chose to support his efforts was John Jay, whom he appointed first Chief Justice of the United States.

Although it is not included in this study, Jay's continued role of public service was significant. He participated in the *Chisholm vs. Georgia* decision, which ruled that the Constitution gave a citizen of one state the right to sue another state. This decision touched off a reaction so intense that it was repudiated almost immediately by the Eleventh Amendment to the Constitution. Yet Jay's contention that the powers of the federal government emanate from the people as a whole rather than from the states was vindicated time and again, particularly by the later Supreme Court arguments of that ardent nationalist on the bench, John Marshall.

While he was still Chief Justice, Jay helped to bring about the downfall of Citizen Genêt, the irrepressible French emissary in America. He was then appointed by Washington as Envoy Extraordinary to England to dissipate the war crisis that had arisen over British occupation of the fur posts in the Northwest Territory and their increasing interference with American commerce. Despite the fact that his position was compromised by Alexander Hamilton's indiscreet communications with the British, Jay finally negotiated a treaty, although one that fell short of guaranteeing American neutral rights. Jay's Treaty, as it was called (although it might be more properly called Hamilton's Treaty), was roundly condemned in this country, and Jay was burned in effigy. After bitter debate the Senate narrowly ratified the treaty, and Washington, convinced by Jay that it was a choice between the treaty and war, signed it. It was a wise decision, for despite its limitations Jay's Treaty prevented a war that this nation was ill-equipped to fight and that might have ended its existence almost before it began. Convinced that he had done his duty, Jay refused to be engulfed by the tide of public criticism that surrounded him and he made no public reply to his critics.

On return from his mission to England, in 1795, he found himself elected Governor of New York. The people of his home state had not forgotten that three years earlier he had been denied the governorship, despite his apparent election. The followers of Governor George Clinton, manipulating the voting canvass with the legal connivance of Aaron Burr, had kept Clinton in office for another term. Despite the fact that he had been elected without his knowledge or consent, Jay resigned from the Supreme Court to assume his new post, and he served two terms with distinction. In this capacity, it was appropriate that as a lifelong critic of slavery he was to sign a bill providing for the eventual end of slavery in New York.

Toward the end of his second term, a notable incident occurred, one that provides a fitting climax to his public career. During the spring elections of 1800, Republicans captured the state legislature, and it was obvious that they would appoint Republican electors for the presidential election in the fall. Hamilton guessed correctly that New York's electoral vote would be crucial, and he importuned Jay to call a special session of the old Federalist legislature for the purpose of amending New York's constitution to have the electors chosen by districts, so gerrymandered as to guarantee the selection of Federalists. Despite the fact that Jay was a staunch Federalist and that he had been savagely abused by the Republicans, he regarded Hamilton's request for what it was — a party measure that clearly conflicted with the will of the people. To accept might prevent the election of Jefferson and Burr, but it meant compromising principle and integrity; he did not even reply to Hamilton, and his silence gave eloquent testimony to his contempt for such endeavors.

In late 1800, without consulting Jay, John Adams appointed his old friend to serve once again as Chief Justice of the Supreme Court. The call was strong, and Jay meditated over it for several days. At the age of fifty-six, however, he was finally determined to retire from public life and share his remaining days with his beloved Sally, who had been ill for several years; he declined the office, an action that led to the sunset of his own political career, but projected John Marshall across the national horizon. His hopes were shattered by the death of Sally the following year, but his deep religious convictions sustained him, as they would continue to do throughout the many years of his retirement until his death, at the age of eighty-three, on May 17, 1829.

Jay's Published Writings and Biographies

Much of Jay's writing was originally edited by his son, William Jay, who, in an apparent effort to demonstrate his father's lack of human frailty, emphasized those materials that illuminated character and virtue and omitted others that might cast him in a controversial light. William also revised the works to eliminate the elder Jay's use of the idiom of his own day: capital letters were dropped to the lower case; changes in spelling were made; commas, semi-colons, colons, and periods were added or subtracted at various points to tighten the mechanics of the writing.

Succeeding biographies in the nineteenth century were written by descendants of John Jay or by those who leaned heavily on the work of William Jay. The most significant work of that period was Henry P. Johnson's four-volume *Correspondence and Public Papers of John Jay* (published 1890–1893), which is a valuable collection of Jay's writing from which much of the source material of this study is drawn, Johnson did not have access to various manuscript materials, however, and omitted passages in certain letters and reports possibly because he did not feel that they were relevant. Until 1965 the only major twentieth-century work on Jay was Frank Monaghan's *John Jay: Defender of Liberty* written in 1935. Monaghan, recognizing the limitations of the previous works, probed into Jay manuscript material, some of which had not been published, particularly the Iselin family collection to which he was given special access. The Iselin material importantly supplemented the Johnson edition, not only because some of it was new, but also because Monaghan wisely chose not to edit Jay into the modern idiom, thereby retaining the original flavor of his writing. The present study draws upon Monaghan's use of this collection.

Professor Richard Morris of Columbia University is now editing an up-to-date collection of the published and unpublished Jay materials in an effort to bring John Jay into sharper focus in American history and historiography. In 1965 Morris published a major work that grew out of his labors called *The Peacemakers: The Great Powers and American Independence;* it is a monumental study of the peace negotiations that ended the Revolutionary War and sharply etches the significant role that Jay played in establishing the independence of the United States. Morris has drawn upon rich source materials for his volume, particularly those only available in overseas archives, and the present study utilizes those valuable sources wherever feasible.

Since Jay's public career was closely associated with those of Washington, Jefferson, Hamilton, Franklin, Madison, and John Adams, the collections of their writings, particularly the more recent editions, have contributed extensively to this study. The most valuable is Professor Julian Boyd's multi-volume *The Papers of Thomas Jefferson,* which contains letters to and from Jefferson in their original form. In the Boyd volumes, Jay's letters to Jefferson appear exactly as Jay wrote them, one of the few places that they do so outside of manuscript form.

The following selections follow the spelling, capitalization, and punctuation of the publications identified in footnotes. Undoubtedly the forthcoming Morris edition of Jay's writings will add many items not now in print, as well as correct flaws in the versions now available.

CHAPTER II

A New York Revolutionary

Until 1774 John Jay did not actively participate in the world of politics, although he, like most New Yorkers, opposed the Stamp Act. The merchants and landowners had encouraged the workers to agitate against this measure to impress British officials, however, the workers organized to become a potent radical and democratizing force. Soon that force would threaten the privileges of the former propertied class, eventually split the political structure of New York, and align the aristocrats or the conservatives against the lower classes or the radicals, sometimes called Sons of Liberty or Liberty Boys.[1]

The New York Tea Party

When Parliament granted a tea monopoly to the East India Company, enabling tea to be sold more cheaply in the colonies than in England, and more cheaply than colonial merchants could sell tea smuggled from Holland, the merchants, with large supplies of tea on hand and their incomes threatened, vigorously protested. Their discontent galvanized the Sons of Liberty into action and resulted in the famous Boston Tea Party in December, 1773. Five months later a lesser known but similar incident occurred in New York. A group of radicals, calling themselves Mohawks, met weekly to prevent tea ships from landing in the province and to threaten violence against merchants who did not cooperate with them. When, in April, 1774, one of the tea ships did not set sail back to England but remained in the harbor, the Mohawks boarded her and dumped the tea overboard.[2]

[1] Carl Becker, The History of Political Parties in the Province of New York, 1760–1776 (Madison: University of Wisconsin Press, 1909), p. 43.

[2] Ibid., p. 110.

8

The Committee of Fifty-one

The action of the Mohawks alarmed many of the conservatives. They were bothered by the violence, but even more importantly by the assumption of more and more influence by extra-legal committees that they did not control; they could not remain aloof any longer if policy was to be directed by moderate men of property rather than by the mob. Their opportunity came when the local chapter of the Sons of Liberty met to protest news of the Port Bill, which had closed Boston Harbor. The radicals formed a special Vigilance Committee to protest the British action and sent a letter on May 15, 1774, to their Boston counterpart:

We have received the shocking and detestable Act of Parliament that shuts up your Port. . . . We want . . . to express our Abhorrence of this additional Act of Tyranny to America . . . a great number of our citizens wish our port to be in the same state with yours. . . . We have stimulated the Merchants to appoint a Meeting tomorrow evening . . . to agree upon a general Non-importation and Non-exportation Agreement of Goods[3]

At the meeting, the merchants, who might be badly hurt by the suggested trade restrictions, turned out in force and succeeded in expanding the committee from twenty-five members to fifty and later to fifty-one. John Jay was one of the men nominated by the merchants, and he was formally elected a few days later. Most of those chosen were men of "sense, coolness and property," giving the conservatives control of the new committee.[4]

[READING NO. 1]
LETTER TO THE COMMITTEE OF CORRESPONDENCE, BOSTON

As a member of the Committee of Fifty-one, Jay was suddenly thrust into the turmoil of the New York political scene. Paul Revere had arrived with an urgent request from the Boston committee to support non-importation. Jay helped draft the cautious reply, which virtually repudiated the earlier letter on non-importation, but did urge joint action by all colonies.

The alarming measures of the British Parliament relative to your ancient and respectable town, which has long been the seat of freedom, fill the inhabitants of this city with inexpressible concern. As a

---

[3] The *Boston Gazette*, May 23, 1774, cited in Frank Monaghan, *John Jay: Defender of Liberty* (New York: The Bobbs-Merrill Co., 1935), pp. 51–52.

[4] Becker, *op. cit.*, pp. 114-115.

sister colony, suffering in defence of the rights of America, we consider your injuries as a common cause, to the redress of which it is equally our duty, and our interest to contribute. But what ought to be done, in a situation so truly critical, while it employs the anxious thoughts of every generous mind, is very hard to be determined.

. . . we conclude that a Congress of Deputies from the colonies in general is of the utmost moment; that it ought to be assembled without delay, and some unanimous resolutions formed in this fatal emergency, not only respecting your deplorable circumstances, but for the security of our common rights. Such being our sentiments, it must be premature to pronounce any judgment on the expedient which you have suggested. We beg, however, that you will do us the justice to believe that we shall continue to act with a firm and becoming regard to American freedom, and to co-operate with our sister colonies in every measure that shall be thought salutary and conducive to the public good.[5]

At the same time this proposal for a general congress provided the Committee of Fifty-one with an honorable way out of a sticky situation, it also was a serious suggestion to consider the common rights of the colonies in general and helped to crystallize sentiment in the other colonies for such a meeting, which took place in Philadelphia a few months later. Meanwhile in New York City the struggle between the radicals and conservatives continued. The Liberty Boys tried to intimidate the local merchants, hoping to force them to accept non-importation anyway, and the conservatives denounced such radical tactics; the Vigilance Committee was pitting its strength against the Committee of Fifty-one. When the former adopted a resolution for non-importation, the latter publicly declared, in July, 1774:

That it is our greatest Happiness and Glory to have been born British Subjects, and that we wish nothing more ardently than to live and die as such; . . . [but] the act for the Blocking up of the port of Boston is . . . subversive to every idea of British Liberty.[6]

---

[5] John Jay, *Correspondence and Public Papers of John Jay*, ed. Henry P. Johnson (New York: G. P. Putnam's Sons, 1890–1893. 4 vols.) I, 13–15. Here and later the original spelling and punctuation have been followed.

[6] *New York Journal*, July 14, 1774, cited in George Pellew, *John Jay* (Boston: Houghton Mifflin and Co., 1890), p. 31.

Non-importation should, however, be left to the proposed congress and justified only by "dire necessity."[7] Despite attempts by the radicals to defeat him, Jay was elected as one of the delegates to this body, joining Philip Livingston, John Alsop, Isaac Low, and James Duane as part of the New York delegation.[8] For the time being, the conservatives had beaten back the radical challenge, although they could not ignore radical sentiment.

The First Continental Congress

When the First Continental Congress assembled in Carpenter's Hall in Philadelphia in September, 1774, Jay was thrust into the company of such men as George Washington, Patrick Henry, Richard Henry Lee of Virginia, John Adams, and Samuel Adams. These were men of great reputation; Jay by contrast, was virtually unknown outside of New York, and his political experience was limited to his work on the Committee of Fifty-one. He did not seem overly awed by this great assemblage, however, and early took issue with Patrick Henry on the crucial matter of how the colonies should vote. John Adams described the episode in his diary:

Mr. Henry . . . arose, and said this was the first general Congress which had ever happened—that no former Congress could be a Precedent—that we should have occasion for more general Congresses, and therefore that a precedent ought to be established now. That it would be great Injustice, if a little Colony should have the same Weight in the Council of America, as a great one, and therefore he was for a Committee.[9]

Then Adams himself commented:

This is a Question of great importance.—If We vote by Colonies, this Method will be liable to great Inequality and Injustice, for 5 small

---

[7] *Ibid.*

[8] Becker, *op. cit.*, pp. 135–141. Twelve colonies sent fifty-six delegates to Philadelphia. Georgia was not represented.
Philip Livingston was a New York merchant and Jay's uncle by marriage; John Alsop was also a New York merchant who, after the Declaration of Independence, refused to take part in public affairs; Isaac Low was also a merchant who later joined the Loyalist cause; James Duane was a lawyer who later became mayor of New York City. Although four other men were elected from other counties, the five New York City delegates were authorized to act for most of the other counties in the state.

[9] John Adams, *Diary and Autobiography of John Adams*, ed. L. H. Butterfield (Cambridge: Harvard University Press, 1961. 3 vols.), II, 123. September 5, 1774.

Colonies, with 100,000 People in each may outrate 4 large ones, each of which has 500,000 Inhabitants. If We vote by the Poll, some Colonies have more than their Proportion of Members, and others have less. If we vote by Interests, it will be attended with insuperable Difficulties, to ascertain the true Importance of each Colony.—Is the Weight of a Colony to be ascertained by the Quantity of their Exports and Imports, or by any component Ratio of both. This will lead us into such a Field of Controversy as will greatly perplex us. Besides I question whether it is possible to ascertain, at this time, the Numbers of our People or the Value of our Trade. It will not do in such a Case, to take each other's Words. It ought to be ascertained by authentic Evidence from Records.[10]

The next day, September 6, 1774, the debate began in earnest when Patrick Henry opened the session with dramatic eloquence, stating the case for a weighted vote according to population:

Government is dissolved. Fleets and Armies and the present State of Things shew that government is dissolved—Where are your Land Marks? your Boundaries of Colonies? We are in a State of Nature, Sir . . . . The Disinctions between Virginians, Pennsylvanians, New Yorkers, and New Englanders, are no more, I am not a Virginian but an American.[11]

Jay was not ready to accept this radical sentiment, and after comments by several others he replied:

Could I suppose that we came to frame an American Constitution, instead of indeavoring to correct faults in an old one—I cant yet think that all Government is at an End. The Measure of arbitrary Power is not yet full, and I think that it must run over, before We undertake to frame a new Constitution.[12]

The matter was resolved that day when the congress voted that since it did not have and could not procure proper materials ascertaining the importance of each colony, "each Colony or Province shall have one Vote."[13]

Jay's moderate approach was again highlighted in his support for the

[10] *Ibid.*, pp. 123–124. September 5, 1774.

[11] *Ibid.*, p. 124–125. September 6, 1774.

[12] *Ibid.*, p. 126. September 6, 1774.

[13] *Ibid.*

plan of Joseph Galloway of Philadelphia, later a leading Loyalist, to restore the rights of the colonies in a permanent union with Great Britain — through joint British–American legislative action involving a council of delegates from the various colonial assemblies. When Richard Henry Lee objected to the plan, Jay answered: "I am led to adopt this Plan. It is objected that this Plan will alter our Constitutions and therefore, cannot be adopted without consulting Constituents. Does this plan give up one Liberty? — or interfere with any one Right."[14]

The delegates defeated Galloway's resolution by a vote of six to five delegations. The mention of it was expunged from the records, but Jay had made his position clear, and the radicals did not like it. John Adams later wrote in his diary the views of Patrick Henry. "He has a horrid Opinion of Galloway, Jay and the Rutledges [of South Carolina]. Their System he says would ruin the Cause of America."[15]

Yet the conservative Jay supported the radical cause when he signed the agreement known as the Association. It was probably the most important action of this Congress, the instrument by which the members stood squarely on the ground of non-importation (and non-exportation) and agreed to implement by boycott and confiscation. An extra-legal body had now become a revolutionary government.

It is doubtful whether the First Continental Congress realized the full impact of what it had done — that this agreement was to become the forerunner of independence. Certainly Jay had not. To him it was a matter of commitment and practicality: the former because he had pledged to make non-importation a matter for Congress to decide, and the majority favored it; the latter because he saw no immediate alternative. "Negociation, suspension of Commerce and War are the only three things. War is, by general Consent, to be waived at present. I am for Negociation and suspension of Commerce."[16] Several days prior to the acceptance of the Association, Jay was appointed, with William Livingston and Richard Henry Lee, to a committee to draw up an address to the people of Great Britain. It was an attempt to make the British people aware of the agonizing position of their counterparts in the colonies. Lee was chosen to write the statement, but Jay was not happy with the Virginian's efforts, and he wrote a rough draft of an address that he felt was more in order. When Lee's proposals were coolly received by Congress, William Livingston read Jay's draft, but did not identify the author.[17] It was a statement of rights, a

[14] *Ibid.,* p. 143. September 28, 1774.
[15] *Ibid.,* p. 151. October 11, 1774.
[16] *Ibid.,* p. 139. September 26–27, 1774.
[17] Monaghan, *op. cit.,* p. 61.

13

criticism of the British ministry, a warning of colonial action, and a plea for understanding and justice, all wrapped together.

[READING NO. 2]

ADDRESS TO THE PEOPLE OF GREAT BRITAIN

When a nation, led to greatness by the hand of liberty . . . descends to the ungrateful task of forging chains for her friends and children; and instead of giving support to freedom, turns advocate for slavery and oppression, there is reason to suspect she has either ceased to be virtuous, or been extremely negligent in the appointment of her rulers.

. . . The cause of *America* is now the object of universal attention. . . . This unhappy country has not only been oppressed, but abused and misrepresented; and the duty we wove to ourselves and posterity, to your interest, and the general welfare of the British empire, leads us to address you on this very important subject.

Know then, That we consider ourselves, and do insist that we are and ought to be as free as our fellow-subjects in Britain, and that no power on earth has a right to take our property from us without our consent.

. . . We believe there is yet much virtue, much justice, and much public spirit in the English nation. To that justice we now appeal. You have been told that we are seditious, impatient of government, and desirous of independence. Be assured that these are not facts but calumnies. Permit us to be as free as yourselves, and we shall ever esteem a union with you to be our greatest glory, and our greatest happiness; we shall ever be ready to contribute all in our power to the welfare of the empire; we shall consider your enemies as our enemies, and your interest as our own.

But if you are determined that your ministers shall wantonly sport with the rights of mankind: if neither the voice of justice, the dictates of the law, the principles of the constitution, or the suggestions of humanity can restrain your hands from shedding human blood in such an impious cause, we must then tell you, that we will never submit to be hewers of wood or drawers of water for any ministry or nation in the world.

. . . we hope that the magnanimity and justice of the British nation will furnish a parliament of such wisdom, independence, and public spirit as may save the violated rights of the whole empire from the devices of wicked ministers and evil counsellors . . . and thereby restore that harmony, friendship, and fraternal affection . . . so ardently wished for by every true and honest American.[18]

Congress responded to the mood of the address: the radicals felt its firmness, the conservatives reacted to its conciliation, and it was passed. Because of the manner in which William Livingston presented it, however, the authorship of the address was not clear. Many believed that Livingston himself was responsible. Richard Henry Lee, apparently hurt by Congress's rejection of his original draft and resentful of Jay's success, if not his moderate views, did little to set the record straight, and Jay was irritated. Jefferson, who called it "a production certainly of the finest in America,[19] was unsure who wrote it; he recounted Jay's indignation over the mix-up at a meeting of Congress in late June, 1775.

I observed Mr. Jay speaking to R. H. Lee and leading him by the button of the coat to me. 'I understand, sir' said he to me, 'that this gentleman informed you, that Governor Livingston drew the Address to the people of Great Britain.' I assured him, at once that I had not received that information from Mr. Lee . . . and after some explanations the subject was dropped. These gentlemen had had some sparring in debate before, and continued ever very hostile to each other.[20]

John Adams commented on the matter in his *Autobiography:*

Mr. Arthur Lee [of Virginia] in London, has heard more insinuation against Mr. Jay as a suspicious Character, and had written to his Brother Richard Henry Lee or to Mr. Samuel Adams or both: and although they were groundless and injurious, as I have no doubt, my Friends had communicated them too indiscreetly, and had spoken of Mr. Jay too lightly. Mr. Lee had expressed doubts whether Mr. Jay composed the Address to the People of Great Britain and ascribed it to his [Jay's] Father in Law Mr. [William] Livingston afterwards Governor of New Jersey. These things had occasioned some Words, and Animosities which Uniting with the great Questions in Congress had some disagreeable Effects. Mr. Jay's great Superiority to Mr. Livingston in the Art of Composition would now be sufficient to decide the question if the latter had not expressly denied having any share in the Address.[21]

[18] Jay, *Correspondence and Papers,* I, 17–31. October 19, 1774.
[19] Thomas Jefferson, *The Writings of Thomas Jefferson,* ed. Paul L. Ford (New York: 1892–1899. 10 vols.), I, 16.
[20] *Letters of Members of the Continental Congress,* ed. Edmund C. Burnett (Washington, D.C.: The Carnegie Institution of Washington, 1921–1936. 8 vols.), I, 157–158. June 26, 1775.
[21] Adams, *Diary and Autobiography,* III, 341.

After issuing several more addresses, the delegates, late in October, 1774, approved John Dickinson's[22] Petition to the King, which indicted the "designing and dangerous men" around George III, but pledged the monarch continued fidelity. ". . . Your royal authority over us and our connexion with Great Britain, we shall always carefully and zealously endeavor to support and maintain."[23] On this conciliatory note the First Continental Congress adjourned, convinced that now it had accomplished much. The appeals had been made, and the Association was ready to apply the necessary pressures to enforce the boycott of the mother country, but in case their grievances were not assuaged, another assembly was scheduled for the following May.

Reaction to the Congress in New York

John Jay returned to New York, his reputation greatly enhanced by his recent contributions to the Congress. Patrick Henry and Richard Henry Lee might be suspicious and hostile, but the radicals in New York were enthusiastic. His support of non-importation had won them over; they elected him to the new Committee of Sixty that supplanted the old Committee of Fifty-one and was charged with enforcing the soon-to-be instituted boycott.

Not all New Yorkers, however, were ecstatic over the new developments. Many felt that it was more desirable to submit to parliamentary measures that they opposed than to be tyrannized by the extra-legal and violent actions of the local committeemen. When the old Provincial Assembly met early in 1775, the conservatives were in control. They disregarded the efforts of Congress and instead sent their own petition to King George. Later they refused to choose delegates for the Second Continental Congress, and word spread in the other colonies that New York might desert the Association. Thomas Jefferson was among those concerned. He wrote a resolution to the Committee of Correspondence in Virginia urging that

they procure authentic information from the Committee of Correspondence for the province of New York. . . . Whether their house of representatives by any vote or votes . . . have deserted the Union with the other American Colonies. . . . Whether the other Colonies are to consider such vote or votes as declaring truly

---

[22] John Dickinson, delegate from Pennsylvania, favored conciliation rather than force. He later authored the second Petition to the King, another attempt at conciliation. Ultimately he voted against the Declaration of Independence as a matter of principle, but he did volunteer for armed service during the war.

[23] *Journals of the Continental Congress, 1774–1789,* ed. Worthington C. Ford and Gaillard Hunt (Washington, D.C.: U.S. Government Printing Office, 1904–1937. 34 vols.), I, 121. October 26, 1774.

the sense of the people of their province in general, and as forming a rule for their future conduct.[24]

In response to this concern from the other colonies, Jay drafted a reassuring letter from the Committee of Sixty, to the Committee of Correspondence in Boston:

the People in general are Zealous in the Cause. . . . Men there are among us, and such there are in every Colony, to whom a Defection would be an agreeable Event, but happily for us this is not the Case with the Bulk of the People. At present little more is to be feared from this Class of Individuals than impotent Invective and illiberal Calumny.[25]

At the special Provincial Convention in April, Jay was chosen as one of his colony's delegates to the Second Continental Congress. The day after the convention dissolved, news arrived of bloodshed at Lexington. New York City erupted in a frenzy of disorder and looting as a mob seized arms and ammunition from the arsenal and grew out of control.[26] The Committee of Sixty felt itself too limited in power and recommended the election of a new Committee of One Hundred with full authority to conduct the government and elect delegates to a Provincial Congress. The old Provincial Assembly had dissolved itself in early April and had never met again, which meant that the reins of government were in the hands of the new group, called the Committee of Observation. For a while mobs continued to roam the city streets, but the radicals threw their support to the committee, and slowly order began to be restored. Jay was an active member of this powerful new body, but as he was also a delegate to the Second Continental Congress, he had to leave for Philadelphia in early May.

The Second Continental Congress

The king had not responded to the petition of the previous Congress, and now blood had been spilled in Massachusetts. The mood of the new Congress was grave. James Duane, a member of the New York delegation, wrote:

[24] Thomas Jefferson, *The Papers of Thomas Jefferson*, ed. Julian P. Boyd (Princeton: Princeton University Press, 1950——. 17+ vols.), I, 159.

[25] Iselin MSS., cited in Monaghan, *op. cit.*, p. 66.

[26] Monaghan, *op. cit.*, p. 67.

The eyes of Europe and America are fixed on this Assembly, and the fate of one of the greatest empires on earth, in no small degree, depends on the issue of their deliberations.[27]

In his *Autobiography* John Adams commented in retrospect:

the Battle of Lexington . . . changed the Instruments of Warfare from the Penn to the Sword. . . . the Die was cast, the Rubicon passed. . . . It appeared to me, that all Petitions, Remonstrances and Negotiations, for the future will be fruitless and only occasion a Loss of time and give Opportunity to the Ennemy to sow divisions among the States and the People. . . . We ought to declare the Colonies, free, Sovereign and independent States, and then inform Great Britain we were willing to enter into Negotiations with them for redress of all Grievances, and a restoration of Harmony between the two Countries, upon Permanent Principles.[28]

The atmosphere of the State House (later known as Independence Hall) was charged with emotion, and Jay was now in the center of activity. No longer the political unknown who had arrived at the first Congress, Jay was chosen to prepare an appeal to the people of Canada. It was not an easy assignment since part of Jay's earlier *Address to the People of Great Britain* had criticized the 1763 Quebec Act's establishment of Catholicism on a favored basis in Canada, an action that he and many others regarded, rightly or wrongly, as threatening the religious liberty of the colonies. Now he had to convince these same people, mostly French Catholics whose religion was guaranteed protection, that their freedom was jeopardized, and invite them to join with the thirteen colonies that were breaking ties with the mother country.

[READING NO. 3]

ADDRESS TO THE OPPRESSED INHABITANTS OF CANADA

Alarmed by the designs of an arbitrary Ministry to extirpate the rights and liberties of all *America,* a sense of common danger conspired with the dictates of humanity is urging us to call your attention, by our late address, to this very important object.

Since the conclusion of the late war, we have been happy in con-

[27] *Letters of Members of the Continental Congress,* I, 98.

[28] Adams, *Diary and Autobiography,* III, 314–315. Adams wrote his autobiography between the years 1802–1807, long after the events he describes were over, and therefore it is not as valid as his diary, in which he recorded events immediately; it is nevertheless still valuable for its insights into the tenor and the principal figures of this time.

sidering you as fellow-subjects; and from the commencement of the present plan for subjugating the Continent, we have viewed you as fellow-sufferers with us. As we were both entitled by the bounty of an indulgent Creater to freedom, and being both devoted by the cruel edicts of a despotick Administration, to common ruin, we perceived the fate of the Protestant and Catholick Colonies to be strongly linked together, and therefore invited you to join with us in resolving to be free, and in rejecting, with disdain, the fetters of slavery, however artfully polished.

We most sincerely condole with you on the arrival of that day, in the course of which the sun could not shine on a single freeman in all your extensive dominion. Be assured that your unmerited degradation has engaged the most unfeigned pity of your sister colonies; and we flatter ourselves you will not, by tamely bearing the yoke, suffer that pity to be supplanted by contempt.

When hardy attempts are made to deprive men of rights bestowed by the Almighty; when avenues are cut through the most solemn compacts for the admission of despotism; when the plighted faith of government ceases to give security to dutiful subjects; and when the insidious stratagems and manoeuvres of peace become more terrible than the sanguinary operations of war, it is high time for them to asserts those rights, and with honest indignation oppose the torrent of oppression rushing in upon them.

By the introduction of your present form of government, or rather present form of tyranny, you and your wives and your children are made slaves. You have nothing that you can call your own, and all the fruits of your labour and industry may be taken from you whenever an avaricious governor and a rapacious council may incline to demand them. You are liable by their edicts to be transported into foreign countries, to fight battles in which you have no interest, and to spill your blood in conflicts from which neither honour nor emolument can be derived. Nay, the enjoyment of your very religion, on the present system, depends on a legislature in which you have no share, and over which you have no control; and your priests are exposed to expulsion, banishment, and ruin, whenever their wealth and possessions furnish sufficient temptation. They cannot be sure that a virtuous Prince will always fill the throne; and should a wicked or careless King concur with a wicked Ministry in exacting the treasure and strength of your country, it is impossible to conceive to what variety and to

19

what extremes of wretchedness you may, under the present establishment, be reduced.

We are informed you have already been called upon to waste your lives in a contest with us. Should you, by complying in this instance, assent to your new establishment, and war break out with *France,* your wealth and your sons may be sent to perish in expeditions against their islands in the West Indies.

It cannot be presumed that these considerations will have no weight with you, or that you are so lost to all sense of honour. We can never believe that the present race of Canadians are so degenerated as to possess neither the spirit, the gallantry, nor the courage of their ancestors. You certainly will not permit the infamy and disgrace of such pusillanimity to rest on your own heads, and the consequences of it on your children forever.

We, for our parts, are determined to live free, or not at all; and we are resolved that posterity shall never reproach us with having brought slaves into the world.

Permit us again to repeat that we are your friends, not your enemies, and be not imposed upon by those who may endeavor to create animosities. The taking of the fort and military stores at *Ticonderoga* and *Crown Point,* and the armed vessels on the lake, was dictated by the great law of self-preservation. They were intended to annoy us, and to cut off that friendly intercourse and communication, which has hitherto subsisted between you and us. We hope it has given you no uneasiness, and you may rely on our assurances that these Colonies will pursue no measures whatever, but such as friendship and a regard for our mutual safety and interest may suggest.

As our concern for your welfare entitles us to your friendship, we presume you will not, by doing us an injury, reduce us to the disagreeable necessity of treating you as enemies.

We yet entertain hopes of your uniting with us in the defence of our common liberty, and there is yet reason to believe, that should we join in imploring the attention of our Sovereign, to the unmerited and unparalleled oppression of his American subjects, he will at length be undeceived, and forbid a licentious Ministry any longer to riot in the ruins of the rights of mankind.[29]

[29] Jay, *Correspondence and Papers,* I, 32–36, May 29, 1775.

The "oppressed inhabitants" of Canada did not feel their position to be quite so perilous, however, and ignored Jay's appeal.

The mood of Congress was growing more bellicose, and Jay, fearing a permanent rupture with the mother country, threw his support to the proposal to send a second petition to the king. After heated debate, Congress appointed Jay to a committee to draw a draft. Although John Dickinson wrote the final document, the measure had Jay's strong support, and he successfully urged it through Congress on July 8, 1775, despite strong opposition.[30]

With the news of British troop movements in Boston ringing in his ears, John Adams felt the Petition to be incongruous with the events of the day and commented in his *Autobiography:*

This Measure of Imbecility, the second Petition to the King embarassed every Exertion of Congress: it occasioned Motions and debates without End for appointing Committees to draw up a declaration of the Causes, Motives and Objects of taking Arms, with a view to obtain decisive declarations against Independence.[31]

While the petition was still in committee, the New York delegates received a letter from the Provincial Congress of New York. Drafted by Gouverneur Morris, it suggested a plan of conciliation that would include a permanent continental congress, a president appointed by the crown, repeal of unpopular parliamentary legislation, and the grant of the power of taxation to colonial assemblies. Failure to resolve the current crisis might in itself lead to greater dangers, and conscience demanded that alternatives to war be explored.

We must now repeat to You, the Common and just Observation that Contests for Liberty, fostered in their Infancy by the virtuous and wise, become Sources of Power to wicked and designing Men. From whence it follows that such Controversies as we are now engaged in, frequently end in the Demolition of those Rights and Privileges, which they were instituted to defend. We pray you therefore to use every Effort for the compromising of this unnatural Quarrel between the Parent and Child . . . so that if even at the last, our well meant Endeavors shall fail of effect, We may stand fair and unreproachable by our own Consciences, in the last solemn appeal to the God of Battles.[32]

The news of Bunker Hill (Breed's Hill) alarmed Congress, and the New York plan was not adopted, but it had mirrored both Jay's hope for re-

---

[30] William Jay, *The Life of John Jay* (New York: J. & J. Harper, 1833. 2 vols.), I, 36.

[31] Adams, *Diary and Autobiography*, III, 321.

[32] Iselin MSS., cited by Monaghan, *op. cit.,* p. 71. June 28, 1775.

conciliation and his growing concern lest continued unrest put too much power in the hands of people who might abuse its use. Congress already had appointed Washington Commander-in-Chief of the Continental Army, but Jay still hoped that compromise was possible.

Congress adjourned for the month of August, 1775, and then returned to Philadelphia in September. Not knowing that in August the king had issued a royal proclamation denouncing the colonists as rebels and declaring that they would be suppressed by force, Jay continued to be optimistic that some form of reconciliation was possible. But John Adams was convinced that action of another kind was necessary:

almost every day, I had something to say about Advizing the States to institute Governments, to express my total despair of any good from the Petition or any of those Things which were called conciliatory measures. I constantly insisted that all such measures, instead of having any tendency to produce Reconciliation, would only be considered proofs of our Timidity and want of Confidence in the Ground We stood on, and would only encourage our Ennemies to great Exertions against Us. That we should be driven to the Necessity of Declaring ourselves independent States.[33]

Adams was not alone. A parliamentary act, restraining commerce, affected nine colonies. New York was not included, but there was strong sentiment to have New York and the other three colonies close their ports, too. Jay was firmly opposed to such action:

Because [the] Ministry have imposed hardships on one, shall we impose the same on all? It is not from affection to New York that I speak. If a man has lost his teeth on one side of his jaws, shall he pull out the teeth from the other, that both sides may be upon a footing? . . . The other Colonies may avail themselves of the custom-houses in the exempted Colonies.[34]

His efforts were in vain; Parliament soon prohibited trade with all the colonies.

Throughout November and December, Congress kept establishing committees, and Jay was appointed to several of them, including the secret committee charged with corresponding "with our friends in Great Britain, in Ireland and other parts of the world." He was troubled, however, that John Adams was not a member of that committee or of the equally im-

[33] Adams, *Diary and Autobiography*, III, 327.
[34] *Journals of the Continental Congress*, III, 492. October 12, 1775.

portant committee on commerce. Knowing the sensitive Adams might be hurt by this slight, Jay sought out the New Englander to soften the blow. Adams recreates the incident in his *Autobiography:*

He said in express terms "that my character stood very high with the Members, and he knew there was but one Thing which prevented me from being universally acknowledged to be the first Man in Congress and that was this, there was a great Division in the House, and two Men had effected it, Samuel Adams and Richard Henry Lee, and I was known to be very intimate with those two Gentlemen, many others were jealous of me."[35]

While Adams tried, almost too modestly, to discount his own importance and reaffirmed his friendship for the other Adams and Lee, he was moved by Jay's sincerity. That night the strong link between the two was forged. As Jay left, Adams recalled: "Mr. Jay and I however parted good Friends and have continued such without interruption."[36]

When the New Jersey Assembly prepared a separate petition to the king in December, 1775, Jay was one of three men sent to dissuade them. As Jay did not date his written comments, there is some dispute as to the time they were written, but, apparently, he took this opportunity to answer the charges that echoed in New Jersey and elsewhere that Congress was striving to achieve independence.[37] He excerpted several passages from the congressional proceedings that recorded attempts to attain reconciliation and included them in a paper—probably for presentation to the New Jersey Assembly. His tone was emphatic.

[READING NO. 4]
EFFORTS OF CONGRESS TO MAINTAIN TIES WITH BRITAIN

It has long been the art of the enemies of America to sow the seeds of Dissensions among us and thereby weaken that union on which our salvation from tyranny depends. For this purpise jealousies have been endeavoured to be executed, and false reports, wicked slanders and insidious misrepresentations industriously formed and propagated.

Well knowing that while the people reposed confidence in the Congress the designs of the ministry would probably be frustrated, no

---

[35] Adams, *Diary and Autobiography,* III, 341.
[36] *Ibid.*
[37] Monaghan *(op. cit.,* p. 442) points out that Johnson's assumption that this paper was written in April, 1775 (Jay, *Correspondence and Papers,* I, 52), is erroneous, because the water marks on the paper Jay used corresponded with those on letters written to his wife in early December, 1775.

pains have been spared to traduce that respectable assembly and misrepresent their designs and actions. Among other aspersions cast upon them, is an ungenerous and groundless charge of their aiming at Independence, or a total separation from G. Britain. Whoever will be at the trouble of reviewing their Journal will find ample testimony against this accusation . . . [In the following material the italics are Jay's.]

Page 63.—The Congress after resolving that the Colonies ought to be put in a state of Defence, thus proceed—"But as *we most ardently wish for a Restoration of the Harmony* formerly subsisting between our mother country and these Colonies, the interruption of whuch must, at all events be exceedingly injurious to both countries, *that with a sincere Design of contributing by all the means in our Power,* (not incompatible with a just regard for the undoubted Rights and true interests of these Colonies) *to the Promotion of their most desirable Reconciliation* an humble and dutiful Petition be presented to his Majesty, Resolved *that measures be entered into for opening a negotiation, in order to accommodate the unhappy Disputes subsisting between Great Britain and these Colonies,* and that *this* be made a *Part of the Petition to the King.*"

Page 64.—The Congress recommend to the Convention of New York "to persevere the more vigorously in preparing for their Defence, as it is very uncertain whether *the earnest endeavours of the Congress to accommodate the unhappy Differences between Great Britain and the Colonies, by conciliatory measures will be successful.*"

Page 84.—The Congress in order to rescue the Province of Massachusetts Bay from anarchy, advise their "Assembly or Council exercise the Powers of Government *until a Governor of his Majesty's appointment will consent to govern the colony according to its charter.* . . ."

Page 149.—The Congress after declaring the Reasons which Compelled them to recur to arms, then express themselves—"Lest this Declaration should disquiet the minds of our friends and fellow subjects in any Part of the Empire, we assure them that *we mean not to dissolve that union which has so long and so happily subsisted between us,* and which we sincerely *wish* to see restored. Necessity has not yet *driven* us into that *desperate* measure, or induced us to excite any other nation to war against them. We *have not* raised armies with *ambitious Designs of separating from Great Britain,* and establishing independent States. . . ."

Page 155.—In the Petition to the King, every line of which breaths affection for his Majesty & Great Britain, are these remarkable sentences:

"Attached to your Majesty's Person, Family, and Government, with all the Devotion that Principle and affection can inspire, *connected with Great Britain by the strongest ties that can unite Societies, and deploring every Event* that lends in *any degree* to *weaken* them, we *solemnly assure* your Majesty, that we not only *most ardently desire* the former *Harmony* between her and these colonies may be *restored*, but that a *Concord* may be *established between them* upon so *firm a basis* as to perpetuate its blessings uninterrupted *by any future Dissentions* to succeeding Generations in both countries." "We beg leave further to assure your Majesty that notwithstanding the *sufferings* of your loyal colonists during the course of this present controversy our Breasts retain *too tender a Regard* for the *Kingdom from which we derive our origin*, to request such a Reconciliation as might in *any manner be inconsistent with her Dignity or welfare*."

Pages 163.—In the last address of the Congress to the People of Great Britain are the following Passages:

"*We are accused of aiming at Independence; but how* is this accusation *supported? by the allegations* of your *ministers*, not by *our actions*. Abused, insulted, and contemned, *what steps have we pursued to obtain Redress? We have carried our dutiful Petitions to the Throne; we have applied to your justice for Relief*."

Page 165.—"Give us leave most solemnly to assure you *that we have not yet lost sight of the object we have ever had in view, a Reconciliation with you on constitutional Principles, and a Restoration of that friendly Intercourse which to the advantage of both, we till lately maintained*."

Page 172.—In the address of the Congress to the Lord Mayor, Aldermen and Livery of London, there is this Paragraph, vizt:

"*North America, my Lords, wishes most ardently for a lasting connection with Great Britain on terms of just and equal liberty*."

From these testimonies it appears extremely evident that to charge the Congress with aiming at a separation of these Colonies from Great Britain, is to charge them falsely and without a single spark of evidence to support the accusations. Many other passages in their Journal might be mentioned, but as that would exceed limits of this paper, I shall reserve them for some future publication.

It is much to be wished that people would read the Proceedings of the Congress and consult their own judgments, and not suffer themselves to be *duped by men who are paid for deceiving them.*[38]

The Provincial Congress of New York, 1776

Meanwhile, Alexander Hamilton[39] sent Jay several letters apprising him of conditions in New York. The royal governor, William Tryon, had fled to a British warship in New York Harbor and tried to administer affairs from there, but the government was in the hands of a Committee of Public Safety, appointed by the Provincial Congress, which had dissolved itself and ordered a new election.[40] Loyalists, however, were trying to restore the force of the old Provincial Assembly and to thwart the Committee. Hamilton hoped that Jay and other New York delegates to Congress might be candidates when local legislative elections were held and urged Jay to return to New York:

It appears to me that as the best way to keep the attention of the people united and fixed to the same point, it would be expedient that four of our Continental delegates should be candidates for this city and county; Mr. [Robert R.] Livingston, Mr. [John] Alsop, Mr. [Francis] Lewis, Mr. Jay. The minds of all our friends will naturally tend to these, and the opposition will of course be weak and contemptible, for the whigs I doubt not constitute a large majority of the people. If you approve the hint, I should wish for your presence here. Absence you know is not very favorable to the influence of any person however great.[41]

Jay could not return at that time, however, as his wife had given birth to a son in early January, and her precarious health demanded his attention. When the new assembly met in February, it was prorogued and accomplished nothing.[42]

Later in April, Jay was elected to the New York Provincial Congress, under authorization of the Committee of Public Safety, which requested that he return for its session. He took leave of Congress in May without officially vacating his seat, apparently intending to return in a few weeks,

[38] Jay, *Correspondence and Papers,* I, 52–56.
[39] Hamilton had interrupted his studies at King's College because of the current political troubles. In 1774 and 1775, when he was about twenty years of age, he wrote pamphlets that took the same moderate position that Jay then held.
[40] Alexander Hamilton, *The Papers of Alexander Hamilton,* ed. Jacob E. Cooke and Harold C. Syrett (New York: Columbia University Press, 1961——. 9+ vols.), I, 179 December 31, 1775.
[41] *Ibid.* Alsop and Lewis were merchants in New York City.
[42] *Ibid.*

but events moved too rapidly, and he became deeply immersed in the activities of his own colony.

At Philadelphia the mood of the Second Continental Congress was steadily growing more angry and resentful toward England. Thomas Paine's *Common Sense,* written in January and circulated widely,[43] eloquently voiced the folly of continued allegiance to England and issued a call to action: ". . . the period of debate is closed. Arms as the last resource [must] decide the contest; the appeal was the choice of the King, and the Continent has accepted the challenge."[44]

Paine was saying boldly what many people were thinking, and his pamphlet made the cause of independence a public concern. Then in late February word came that, in December, Parliament had followed in the King's footsteps and issued the Prohibitory Bill, which interdicted all trade with the colonies and denounced as rebels and traitors all Americans who did not unconditionally submit to parliamentary authority. Commissioners were empowered to come from England to inquire into grievances and and to receive submissions. To most of the delegates this action was decisive; the earlier royal proclamation was only a proclamation, but Parliament was the supreme legal authority in England, and its action made independence virtually inevitable. Even Jay's friend and fellow New York delegate, Robert R. Livingston — a man who, possessed of considerable wealth, stood to lose much in vulnerable New York — remarked sardonically that the only commissioners that could be expected were the "34,000 commissioners" of the British and mercenary armies.[45]

The Declaration of Independence

For a few months debate continued, but independence was in the air; one could almost feel its presence. John Adams finally took the bull by the horns and recommended that the colonies assume the full powers of government. Although there was still conservative opposition to such drastic action, the resolution was accepted. Adams reflected on the event:

Opposition was made to it, and Mr. Duane called it a Machine to fabricate independence but . . . it passed. It was indeed on all hands considered by Men of

---

[43] Perhaps as many as 300,000 copies were printed. A work, published today, would need more than thirteen million copies to reach a comparable percentage of the population. *Common Sense* may have been the most extraordinary best seller in American history. Howard Fast, *The Selected Work of Tom Paine* (New York: Random House, 1943), p. 40.

[44] *Ibid.,* p. 18.

[45] George Dangerfield, *Chancellor Robert R. Livingston of New York, 1746–1813* (New York: Harcourt, Brace and World, 1960), p. 72.

Understanding as equivalent to a declaration of Independence: tho a formal declaration of it was still opposed by Mr. Dickinson and his Party.[46]

Duane objected, but Jay approved and hoped that New York would form a new government.

In June, Richard Henry Lee, acting on the recommendation of the Virginia Convention, proposed virtually to sever what was left of the imperial cord. In a session of Congress he moved:

That these United Colonies are and ought to be, free and independent states, that they are absolved from all allegiance to the British Crown, and that all political connection between them and the State of Great Britain is, and ought to be, totally dissolved.[47]

Jefferson's notes on the proceedings reveal the dramatic situation that debates on the resolutions created. Livingston, now the leader of the New York delegation, was in a delicate position, and with others he protested:

That some [Colonies] had expressly forbidden their delegates to consent to such a declaration. . . . That if such a declaration should now be agreed to these delegates must retire & possibly their colonies might secede from the Union. . . . On the other side it was argued by J. Adams, [R. H.] Lee, [George] Wythe and others. . . . That the question was not whether, by a declaration of independence, we should make ourselves what we are not; but whether we should declare a fact which already exists:

. . . . That as to the king, we had been bound to him by allegiance, but that this bond was now dissolved by his assent to the late act of Parliament (Prohibitory Act), by which he declares us out of his protection, and by his levying war on us, a fact which had long ago proved us out of his protection; it being a certain position in law that allegiance & protection are reciprocal, the one ceasing when the other is withdrawn.[48]

As the debates continued, it was clear to Jefferson that New York and other colonies

. . . were not yet matured for falling from the parent stem, but that they were fast advancing to that state, it was thought most prudent to wait a while for them, and to postpone the final decision to July 1. but that this might occasion as little delay as possible, a committee was appointed [on June 11] to prepare a declaration

[46] Adams, *Diary and Autobiography,* III, 335.
[47] *Journals of the Continental Congress,* V, 388. June 7, 1776.
[48] Jefferson, *Papers,* I, 310–311. June 7, 1776.

of independence. the Commee. were J. Adams, Dr. Franklin, Roger Sherman, Robert R. Livingston & myself.[49]

Before Livingston was appointed to this significant committee, he had written, on June 8, 1776, in the name of the entire delegation, a letter to the New York Provincial Congress asking for new instructions. No one, he said, knew how to vote on these resolutions, and some felt they had no right to vote at all.[50] In debating Livingston's letter, the Provincial Congress actually passed a resolution, proposed by John Jay, that the electors invest their deputies with the right to declare New York independent, but they agreed not to publish the resolution until after the approaching election for a new legislative body, thus making it impossible for the people to express themselves on independence in a way that was binding on their delegation in Philadelphia.[51] Instead, on June 11, 1776, they unanimously approved another of Jay's resolutions planned to avoid the division in the forthcoming election.

[READING NO. 5]

NEW YORK'S REFUSAL TO ENDORSE INDEPENDENCE

The good people of this colony have not, in the opinion of this Congress, authorized this Congress, or the Delegates of this Colony in the Continental Congress, to declare this Colony to be and continue independent of the Crown of Great Britain.[52]

The New York decision was communicated to the delegates in Philadelphia. It was clear to Livingston that "no steps inconsistent with their intention" might be taken until the election of the new Provincial Congress.[53] Perhaps he thought about the situation in New York as he sat on the committee working on a declaration of independence. Although Adams and Jefferson later disagreed on the circumstances in which Jefferson was chosen to write the draft of the declaration, it is evident that only Adams and Franklin emended the draft, and it is equally clear that for whatever

---

[49] *Ibid.,* p. 313. June 28, 1776.

[50] Dangerfield, *op. cit.,* p. 76.

[51] *Ibid.,* p. 76. This matter may not have been crucial. Monaghan *(op. cit.,* p. 82) points out that the ultra-conservatives refused to participate and withdrew, leaving the new congress wholly a revolutionary group.

[52] *Journals of the Provincial Congress, Provincial Convention Committee of Safety and Council of Safety of the State of New York, 1775–1777* (Albany: T. Weed, New York State Printer, 1842. 2 vols.), I, 462.

[53] Dangerfield, *op. cit.,* p. 77.

reason, "Livingston sat in silence among the immortals" on the momentous occasion.[54]

In New York Jay was caught on the horns of a dilemma. His influence in the patriot cause was growing. The Provincial Congress, alarmed at openly pro-British activities, had created a Committee to Detect Conspiracies, with Jay as chairman, which had the power to seize, try, and sentence. This committee discovered a plot against the life of Washington, which resulted in the hanging of Thomas Hickey, one of Washington's soldiers, as a lesson to potential conspirators.[55] Because of Jay's importance to the state, the new Provincial Congress had directed him not to leave New York without further orders. At the same time the conservatives still looked to Jay for leadership. Edward Rutledge wrote from Philadelphia that Lee's resolution on independence was soon to be acted upon and urged Jay to attend to oppose it.[56] Not yet convinced that independence should be formalized, Jay's answer to Rutledge was sympathetic, but he chose not to leave his state.[57] What his course of action might have been had he gone to Philadelphia is a matter of conjecture, but Jay's decision to remain in New York whether he realized it or not, wedded him to independence. His reaction a few days later, highlighted this commitment. While he was absent from New York City on personal business, a British fleet with General Howe's forces anchored off Sandy Hook, and as a result the Provincial Congress discreetly voted to adjourn and assemble at White Plains on July eighth. When informed of the decision, Jay realizing that this action might be interpreted as a cowardly one, wrote angrily to Livingston: "This precipitate ill-advised Retreat I fear will not be a little injurious to the publick."[58]

On July second, the New York delegates to the Second Continental Congress wrote for new instructions as the vote on independence was imminent. The Provincial Congress had adjourned, however, and the letter was held until their meeting in White Plains.

When the Provincial Congress met on July ninth, the members received not only this letter, but also another that enclosed a copy of the Declaration of Independence. Both letters were referred to a committee of which Jay was chairman. No longer was independence an illusion. The Provincial Congress had to face the fact that twelve states had accepted Lee's resolution in Philadelphia on July second. Would New York refuse to go along?

Whatever the motives in moving to White Plains, the Provincial Con-

[54] *Ibid.*, p. 79.
[55] Monaghan, *op. cit.*, p. 82.
[56] Jay, *Correspondence and Papers*, I, 66–68. July 1, 1776.
[57] *Ibid.*, pp. 68–70.
[58] Iselin MSS., cited in Monaghan, *op. cit.*, p. 83.

gress, through its spokesman, John Jay, with firmness and courage now joined New York to her sister colonies.[59] Jay's resolution, which was unanimously adopted, stated:

[READING NO. 6]
NEW YORK'S ADOPTION OF THE DECLARATION OF INDEPENDENCE

Resolved, unanimously, That the reasons assigned by the Continental Congress for declaring the *United Colonies* free and independent States, are cogent and conclusive; and that while we lament the cruel necessity which has rendered that measure unavoidable, we approve the same, and will, at the risk of our lives and fortunes, join with the other colonies in supporting it.

Resolved, That a copy of the said Declaration, and the aforegoing Resolution, be sent to the Chairman of the Committee of the County of Westchester, with orders to publish the same with beat of drum at this place, on Thursday next, and to give directions that it be published with all convenient speed in the several districts within the said county, and that copies thereof be forthwith transmitted to the other County Committees within the State of *New York,* with orders to cause the same to be published in the several districts of their respective counties.

Resolved, That five hundred copies of the Declaration of Independence, with the two last-mentioned Resolutions of this Congress for approving and proclaiming the same, be published in handbills, and sent to all the County Committees in this State.

Resolved, That the Delegates of this State in Continental Congress, be, and they are hereby, authorized to consent to and adopt all such measures as they may deem conducive to the happiness and welfare of the *United States of America.*[60]

It is questionable whether the moderates led by Jay looked upon this act as an irreparable breach; it is possible that they regarded it as a way to pressure Great Britain into a thorough redress of grievances and the granting of more self-government. If that is true, the course of events was to

[59] Only 25 miles away the British fleet of 130 ships, carrying 14,000 troops was anchored, and to the north across from Lake Champlain, 13,000 troops were poised ready to strike at New York. Monaghan, *op. cit.,* p. 84.
[60] Jay, *Correspondence and Papers,* I, 72–73.

change their outlook. New York, vulnerable to the massing British military forces, later became a bitter battle ground, thus hardening the resolve and determination of these moderate men. In the days and months ahead, most of them would slowly see that there was no other alternative to total separation, and one of them, John Jay, would play a vital role in the achieving of full independence.

CHAPTER III

A Founder
of the State of New York

On July 9, 1776, in New York City, George Washington ordered the Declaration of Independence read to his men and reminded every officer and soldier

. . . to act with Fidelity and Courage . . . knowing that now the peace and safety of his Country depends (under God) solely on the success of our arms: And that he is now in the service of a State possessed of sufficient power to reward his merit and advance him to the highest Honors of a free Country.[1]

In New York, however, the task of implementing independence and establishing "sufficient power" was formidable.

[READING NO. 7]
NEW YORK VS. THE PHILADELPHIA CONGRESS

The day after the Provincial Congress voted independence, Jay wrote a letter to the Second Continental Congress, illustrating the difficulty of overlapping authority between the two bodies. The Philadelphia body had promoted officers in the New York regiment, but in the process many of the older officers had been neglected and had protested the action. As spokesman for the Provincial Congress, Jay intervened. He took particular exception to the assertion that the situation necessitated the action:

The *Necessity of the Case* has in all Ages & Nations of the World been a fruitful tho dangerous Source of Power. It has often sown

---

[1] George Washington, *The Writings of George Washington,* ed. John C. Fitzpatrick (Washington: United States Government Printing Office, 1931–1944. 39 vols.), V, 245.

Tares in the fair Fields of Liberty and like a malignant Blast deystroyed the Fruits of Patriotism & public Spirit. . . . We believe the Congress went into this Measure with pure Intentions . . . we entertain too high an opinion of their Virtue & Integrity to apologize for a Plainess of Speech becoming Freemen & which we know can give offence only to that counterfeit & adulterated Dignity which swells the Pride of those who instead of lending borrow a consequence from their offices.— And Sir we beg Leave to assure Congress that tho we shall always complain & oppose their Resolutions when they injure our Rights [but] we shall ever be ready (however callumniated by Individuals whose Censure we consider as Praise) to risque our Lives and Fortunes in supporting the American Cause.[2]

The New York Loyalists and the Committee on Conspiracies

Defeating the enemy in the field was a herculean task in itself, but it was rendered even more difficult by the machinations of the many active Loyalists or Tories. Although they existed in considerable numbers through-out the state, Queens County, on Long Island, was the center of their activity.[3] Hundreds moved southward to this area to gain British protection, and schemed to gain control of the state.

Many New Yorkers joined the Loyalist camp with enthusiasm; others did so reluctantly. If the British should prevail, the Loyalists stood to reap a profit in power, influence, or financial security. The Declaration of Independence had obliterated the middle ground and forced those who had not committed themselves in the struggle to choose between remaining British subjects, and thus becoming traitors to the new nation, or declaring themselves Americans and hence traitors to the crown. Independence demanded a decision. Some joined the patriot cause. Others, although they considered themselves American, cast their lot with the Tories and found themselves inconsistently accepting British restrictions to which they were basically opposed because they wanted redress in legal ways; they were not rebels!

Whatever the motivation of the Tories, their activities jeopardized the security of the state. To combat this internal threat, John Jay, who had

---

[2] Iselin MSS., cited in Monaghan, *John Jay: Defender of Liberty* (New York: The Bobbs-Merrill Company, 1935), p. 87.

[3] The major work on Loyalist activity is Alexander C. Flick's *Loyalism in New York During the American Revolution* (New York: Columbia University Press, 1901); however, a briefer but equally valuable account is Alexander C. Flick, "The Loyalists," in *History of the State of New York*, ed. Alexander C. Flick (New York: Columbia University Press, 1933–1937. 10 vols.), III, 327–360.

served on the earlier Committee to Detect Conspiracies, was appointed by the legislature as one of the original members of a new state committee with wide powers for "detecting and defeating all conspiracies."[4] Now free and independent, New York was in a position to define treasonable actions, and this committee was responsible for the seizure and trial of those persons engaged in "making war against the state."[5] Prior to the acceptance of the Declaration of Independence, the treatment of Loyalists had been firm but moderate. Some were imprisoned and others exiled from New York, but most were released on their own parole, although restricted in their movements. Both Washington and John Adams complained at such leniency, but the Provincial Congress, through the efforts of Jay and others, was determined to follow a legal and orderly procedure. When local committees acted without authority, triggering mob violence and destruction of property, the legislature denounced and reprimanded them.[6]

But with independence declared and the British occupying the southern part of the state, the matter of security was crucial. Leniency became intolerable for it was a sign of weakness and vacillation; the creation of an impression of strength and determination was essential.

[READING NO. 8]

JAY'S ATTITUDE TOWARD THE LOYALISTS

Jay, secretary and acting chairman of the new committee on conspiracies, stated the committee's purpose in emphatic terms:

Whereas certain inhabitants and subjects of this State, either seduced or corrupted by the bribes of the enemy, or influenced by unmanly fear, profess to owe allegiance to the King of Great Britain, although the said King has denied them his protection, absolved them from their allegiance, and by force of arms attempted to reduce them from subjects to vassals, and from freemen to slaves. . . . Resolved, that the committee appointed by the Convention of this State [shall] have full power and authority to disfranchise and punish all such unworthy subjects of this State . . . by transporting them with their families, at their own expense, to the city of New-York or other places in possession of the enemy; . . . that they who ignominiously prefer servitude

---

[4] *Ibid.*, pp. 348–349.
[5] *Ibid.*, p. 348.
[6] *Ibid.*, pp. 344–345.

to freedom, may, by becoming vassals and slaves to the king and parliament, deter others from the like shameful and dishonourable conduct.[7]

The committee heard many cases and exiled hundreds of Loyalists, including Jay's close friend and college classmate, Peter Van Schaack, who was sent to Boston and later to England. Years later, in a letter to Van Schaack, Jay, although he wrote with affection to his old friend, made it clear that there had been no room for equivocation:

As an Independent American I considered all who were not for us, and you amongst the rest, as against us. . . . No man can serve two masters. Either Britain was right and America was wrong, or America was right and Britain was wrong. . . . I have adhered to certain fixed principles, and faithfully obeyed their dictates without regarding the consequences of such conduct to my friends, my family or myself: all of whom however dreadful the thought, I have ever been ready to sacrifice, if necessary, to the public objects in the contest.[8]

[READING NO. 9]

JAY'S PLAN FOR BLOCKING THE UPPER HUDSON

The strategic location of the new state made it an inviting target. If the English could possibly take and hold Manhattan Island and seize firm control of the Hudson River–Lake Champlain complex, New York would be divided and New England successfully isolated from the other colonies. While the "divide and conquer" campaign eventually failed at Saratoga, British forces soon gained possession of New York City and obtained a base for military operations during most of the Revolution. As a result, much fighting occurred on state soil, especially during the first two years of the war.[9]

That Jay was prepared to make personal sacrifices seems clear in a letter he wrote to Robert Morris, a Philadelphia merchant, in which he advocated extreme measures in the southern part of the state, which if carried out, would have meant the loss of his own property:

Should [the enemy] . . . be able suddenly to penetrate the North River with a few ships of war and a number of transports, they would effec-

---

[7] William Jay, *The Life of John Jay* (New York: J. & J. Harper, 1833. 2 vols.), I, 49–50.

[8] *Correspondence and Public Papers of John Jay,* ed. Henry P. Johnson (New York: G. P Putnam's Sons, 1890–1893. 4 vols.), II, 343–345.

[9] Hoffman Nickerson, "New York and the Strategy of the Revolution," in Flick, ed., *The History of the State of New York,* IV, 75.

tually destroy all communications between the upper country and the army by land and water. For before the shores would be put in such a state of defence as to prevent their landing with success, they might possess themselves of Posts and Passes, by nature so strong as to be long tenable against a much superior force.

Should an event of this sort take place, we should be in a disagreeable situation. Flour and lumber could not then be carried to the army but by a circuitous route thro abominable roads, and it is a matter of some doubt whether our utmost exertions to supply them would be successful. Had I been vested with absolute power in this State, I have often said and still think that I would last spring have desolated all Long Island, Staten-Island, the City and County of New York, and all that part of the County of Westchester which lies below the mountains. I would then have stationed the main body of the army in the mountains on the east, and eight or ten thousand men in the highlands on the west side of the river. I would have directed the river at Fort Montgomery,* which is nearly at the southern extremity of the mountains to be so shallowed as to afford only depth sufficient for an Albany sloop, and all the southern passes and defiles in the mountains to be strongly fortified. Nor do I think the shallowing of the river a romantic scheme. Rocky mountains rise immediately from the shores. The breadth is not very great though the depth is. But what cannot eight or ten thousand men well worked effect? According to this plan of defence the State would be absolutely impregnable against all the world on the Sea side, and would have nothing to fear except from the way of the lake. Should the enemy gain the river even below the mountains, I think I foresee that a retreat would become necessary, and I can't forbear wishing that a desire of saving a few acres may not lead us into difficulty. Such is the situation of this State at present and so various and I may say successful have been the arts of Gov. Tryon and his adherents to spread the seeds of disaffection among us that I cannot at present obtain permission to return to Congress. Our Convention continues unanimous in all its measures and to do them justice are diligent as well as zealous in the cause.[10]

---

* Fort Montgomery was located four miles below West Point and together with nearby Fort Clinton was a key to the Hudson River defenses.

[10] Jay, *Correspondence and Papers*, 86–88. October 6, 1776.

Despite the efforts of Jay and others to maintain internal security, the situation was growing more precarious. While Washington retreated through New Jersey and the British retained firm control of southern New York, Loyalists in the New York City area became bolder and more numerous. Many, who had been passive patriots, repudiated their new allegiance, wore a red ribbon in their hats, and took the oath of loyalty to the crown.

[READING NO. 10]

PATRIOT MORALE: JAY'S ADDRESS

In this dark hour, when it was necessary to rally the spirit of the patriots, to give them renewed faith in themselves and their cause, Jay was asked to frame an appeal to the people of his state. The resulting "Address of the Convention of the Representatives of the State of New York to their Constituents" was a brilliant mixture that included an historical analysis of freedom, a denunciation of British policies, and a call to the true patriot to stand firm against the pressures that sought to enslave him:

You and all men were created free, and authorized to establish civil government, for the preservation of your rights against oppression, and the security of that freedom which God hath given you, against the rapacious hand of tyranny and lawless power. It is therefore, not only necessary to the well-being of Society, but the duty of every man, to oppose and repel all those, by whatever name or title distinguished, who prostitute the powers of Government to destroy the happiness and freedom of the people over whom they may be appointed to rule.

Under the auspices and direction of Divine Providence, your forefathers removed to the wilds and wilderness of America. By their industry they made it a fruitful, and by their virtue a happy country. And we should still have enjoyed the blessings of peace and plenty, if we had not forgotten the source from which these blessings flowed; and permitted our country to be contaminated by the many shameful vices which have prevailed among us . . . .

You may remember that to obtain redress of the many grievances to which the King and Parliament of Great Britain had subjected you, the most dutiful petitions were presented, not only by the several Assemblies, but by the Representatives of all America in General Congress. And you cannot have forgot with what contempt they were neglected; nay, the humblest of all petitions, praying only to be heard, was answered by the sound of the trumpet and the clashing of arms. This, however, is not the only occasion on which the hearts of kings have been hardened; and in all probability it will add to the number of those instances in which their oppression, injustice and hardness of heart have worked their destruction.

Being bound by the strongest obligations to defend the inheritance which God hath given us, to Him we referred our Cause, and opposed the assaults of our taskmasters, being determined rather to die free than live slaves and entail bondage on our children . . . .

The enemy . . . invade us—invade us not less by their arts than their arms. They tell you that if you submit you shall have protection; that their king breathes nothing but peace; that he will revise (not repeal) all his cruel acts and instructions, and will receive you into favour. But what are the terms on which you are promised peace? Have you heard of any except absolute, unconditional obedience and servile submission? . . .

If the British king really desires peace, why did he order all your vessels to be seized, and confiscated? Why did he most cruelly command, that the men found on board such vessels should be added to the crews of his ships of war, and compelled to fight against their own countrymen—to spill the blood of their neighbours and friends; nay, of their fathers, their brothers and their children; and all this before these pretended ambassadors of peace had arrived on our shores! Does any history, sacred or profane, record any thing more horrid, more impious, more execrably wicked, tyrannical or devilish? If there be one single idea of peace in his mind, why does he order your cities to be burned, your country to be desolated, your brethren to starve, and languish, and die in prison? If any thing were intended besides destruction, devastation, and bloodshed, why are the mercenaries of Germany transported near four thousand miles to plunder your houses; ravish your wives and daughters; strip your infant children; expose whole families naked, miserable, and forlorn, to want, to hunger, to inclement skies, and wretched deaths? If peace were not totally reprobated by him, why are those pusillanimous, deluded, servile wretches among you, who, for present ease or impious bribes, would sell their liberty, their children, and their souls; who like savages, worship every devil that promises not to hurt them; or obey any mandates, however cruel, for which they are paid? how is it, that these sordid, degenerate creatures, who bow the knee to this king, and daily offer incense at his shrine,

39

should be denied the peace so repeatedly promised them? Why are they indiscriminately abused, robbed, and plundered, with their more deserving neighbours? But in this world, as in the other, it is right and just that the wicked should be punished by their seducers.

In a word, if peace was the desire of your enemies, and humanity their object, why do they thus trample under foot every right and every duty, human and divine? Why, like the demons of old, is their wrath to be expiated only by human sacrifices? Why do they excite the savages of the wilderness to murder our inhabitants and exercise cruelties unheard of among civilized nations? No regard for religion or virtue remains among them. Your very churches bear witness of their impiety; your churches are used without hesitation as jails, as stables, and as houses of sport and theatrical exhibitions. What faith, what trust, what confidence, can you repose in these men, who are deaf to the call of humanity, dead to every sentiment of religion, and void of all regard for the temples of the Lord of Hosts?

And why all this desolation, bloodshed, and unparalleled cruelty? They tell you to reduce your obedience. Obedience to what? To their will and pleasure! And then what? Why, then you shall be pardoned, because you consent to be slaves. And why should you be slaves now, having been freemen ever since this country was settled? Because, forsooth, the king and parliament of an island three thousand miles off, choose that you should be hewers of wood and drawers of water for them. And is this the people whose proud domination you are taught to solicit? Is this the peace which some of you so ardently desire? For shame! for shame! . . .

If then, God hath given us freedom, are we responsible to him for that, as well as other talents? If it be our birthright, let us not sell it for a mess of pottage, nor suffer it to be torn from us by the hand of violence! . . .

Rouse, therefore, brave Citizens! Do your duty like men! and be persuaded that Divine Providence will not permit this Western World to be involved in the horrours of slavery. . . .

But if there be any among us, dead to all sense of honour, and love of their country; if deaf to all the calls of liberty, virtue, and religion; if forgetful of the magnanimity of their ancestors, and the happiness of their children; if neither the examples nor the success of other nations, the dictates of reason and of nature, or the great duties they owe to their God, themselves, and their posterity, have any effect upon them; if neither the injuries they have received, the prize they are contending for, the future blessings or curses of their children, the applause or the reproach of all mankind, the approbation or displeasure of the Great Judge, or the happiness or misery consequent upon their conduct, in this and a future state, can move them;—then let them be assured, that they deserve to be slaves, and are entitled to nothing but anguish and tribulation. . . .

But we think better things of you. We believe, and are persuaded, that you will do your duty like men, and cheerfully refer your cause to the great and righteous Judge. If success crown your efforts, all the blessings of Freedom will be your reward. If you fail in the contest, you will be happy with God and Liberty in Heaven.[11]

References in the address to the Creator, freedom, liberty, and virtue, touched emotional chords. The statement received enthusiastic response not only in New York but in the Second Continental Congress, which voted that it be translated into German and a thousand copies printed and circulated widely in Pennsylvania and New Jersey.[12]

A New State Constitution for New York

The day after the Provincial Congress voted for independence, it renamed itself the Convention of the Representatives of the State of New York. The name was portentous; it heralded the creation of a new structure of government.

TRANSITIONAL STATE GOVERNMENT

As successive challenges weakened royal authority in the decade 1766–1776, the grievance committees had expanded as a spontaneous extra-legal system to fill the void, and the old Provincial Congress had leaned heavily on them in order to execute policy.[13] Members of the committees were elected through the medium of extra-legal meetings or ballots by land holders—or freeholders, as they were called—to whom the committees were solely responsible. Although by no means truly representative, the extra-legal committees introduced a powerful democratizing influence in New York during the revolutionary period. As the struggle for state power between conservatives and radicals had become more intense, many

[11] Ibid., pp. 102–120.
[12] Monaghan, op. cit., p. 93.
[13] Hugh M. Flick, "The Rise of the Revolutionary Committee System," in Flick, ed., History of the State of New York, III, 211. For additional details see pp. 211–250.

abuses developed under this system, and excesses continued at an even higher level once independence was declared. Still, the committee system provided a partial solution to the immense problem of transition from royal colony to sovereign state; it not only carried on the propaganda that helped to produce the war and materially contributed to the success in winning it, but became the training school for new political leaders.

In the absence of a constitution, the Convention, when its members could meet, governed the state. It functioned as a unicameral legislature; its committees discharged executive and administrative responsibilities. In the intervals when its members could not meet, the Committee of Safety acted for the Convention.[14]

COMMITTEE TO DRAFT A CONSTITUTION, 1776–1777

Independence necessitated a new framework—a state government based on a constitution, with legal powers to make, enforce, and interpret laws and to ensure the rights that the people were struggling against England to preserve. As early as August, 1776, the Committee of Thirteen, including John Jay, was appointed to form a new government. The grave military situation, however, forced the Convention to change its meeting place several times and prevented Jay and other key members of that committee from beginning their task.[15] On several occasions the Convention requested that Jay and his fellow committee members, Robert R. Livingston and Robert Yates, who were absent supervising the fortification of the Hudson, proceed as soon as possible to carry out their committee function to propose a form of government. The military situation was still precarious, however, and despite deadlines set by the Convention, no report was forthcoming for several months, suggesting that there was much truth to the adage of the day, "that it would be well to secure a state to govern, before they discussed a form to govern it by."[16]

Possibly the delay was advantageous to the more conservative forces in the state for there was a strong division in the views of how the state should be governed—an obvious gap existed between a Gouverneur Morris, "the aristocrat," and a John Morin Scott of "the mobility"—as the lower classes were described by Morris.[17] When the committee did meet in February of 1777, Abraham Yates, chairman of the Albany Com-

[14] Ernest W. Spaulding, "The State Government under the First Constitution," in Flick ed., *History of the State of New York*, IV, 154–155.
[15] The convention met at White Plains, Harlem, Kingsbridge, Philipse's Manor, Fishkill, Poughkeepsie, and Kingston, avoiding seizure by British troops (Pellew, *op. cit.,* p. 65)
[16] Spaulding, *op. cit.,* p. 155.
[17] *Ibid.,* p. 156. Morris was a lawyer and member of a prominent New York City family. Scott, also a lawyer in the city, had helped organize the New York Sons of Liberty.

mittee of Correspondence, who represented the more radical majority, was elected chairman, but the conservatives maintained power in the actual drafting of the constitution.

JAY'S ROLE

Who actually wrote the draft that was presented to the Convention on March twelfth is not clear. William Jay gives his father the major credit, remembering that the elder Jay retired to the country to develop a plan of government and indicating that the original report of the committee was in Jay's handwriting.[18] However, that copy of the report is not extant today.[19] John Adams, writing years later to Jefferson to explain Jay's absence from the Second Continental Congress, credits Jay and, indirectly, himself with a vital role in framing New York's constitution:

His absence was accidental. Congress on the 15th of May preceding, as I remember, had recommended to all States to abolish all authority under the crown, and institute and organize a new government under the authority of the people. Mr. Jay had promoted this resolution in New York, by advising them to call a convention to frame a new constitution. He had been chosen a member of that convention, and called home by his constituents to assist in it, and as Duane [of New York] told me, he had gone home with my letter to Wythe [of Virginia] in his pocket, for his model and foundation; and the same Duane, after the Constitution appeared, asked me if it was not sufficiently conformable to my letter to Wythe. I assured him, I believed it would do very well.[20]

The finished constitution did contain some of Adams' suggestions in his letter to Wythe, which was published under the title *Thoughts on Government,* but others were omitted.[21] Precisely how much influence Adams had on Jay or any of the others in New York is impossible to say, but it seems likely that they depended more directly on their knowledge of the British system and the philosophy of Locke and Montesquieu, tempered in the forge of their colonial experiences, than on the advice of the New Englander.

Two drafts exist among the papers of the Convention, but neither is in Jay's handwriting, and the incomplete draft in the Yates papers is in the handwriting of Abraham Yates and Robert R. Livingston.[22] Handwriting,

---

[18] W. Jay, *op. cit.,* I, 69.

[19] Monaghan, *op. cit.,* p. 443.

[20] John Adams, *The Works of John Adams,* ed. Charles Francis Adams (Boston: Little, Brown and Co., 1850–1856. 10 vols.), X, 410–411.

[21] Spaulding, *op. cit.,* p. 157.

[22] *Ibid.*

however, may not be conclusive when determining authorship. It is generally agreed that Jay played a leading role in the drafting of the constitution and that Livingston and Gouverneur Morris were his chief advisors.[23]

Because of the illness of his mother, Jay was not present when his friend Duane read the draft to the Convention on March 12, 1777, but he did take part in the debates during the following month. He clashed with his friend Morris on at least two issues. He proposed that Roman Catholics should not enjoy civil rights until they had sworn that no foreign authority, including the pope, could absolve them of their allegiance to the state; Morris vigorously and successfully opposed him.[24] It seems clear, however, that Jay's motives were not so much those of the bigot as of the skeptic; his Huguenot background and his work on the committtees for detecting conspiracies made him sensitive to potential dangers, and he may have viewed his proposal as a way to remove a possible internal threat. There is no evidence that indicates that Jay was opposed either to religious tolerance in general or to the section of the state constitution in particular, which guarantees "the free exercise and enjoyment of religious profession and worship without discrimination or preference." On the other matter Jay proposed to substitute secret ballot voting for *viva voce* (by voice) voting, the system by which landlords had maintained control over their tenants. Now it was Gouverneur Morris' turn to object; in vain he strenuously opposed the new system which according to Jay "would tend more to preserve the liberty and equal freedom of the people."[25]

A CONSERVATIVE FRAMEWORK

After debating the proposed draft section by section, making changes when they deemed it necessary, the Convention on April 20, 1777, adopted the constitution.[26] The finished document created a two-house legislature. Members of the lower house or Assembly were to be elected principally by freeholders, or landowners, and the Albany and New York "freemen" (merchants, tradesmen, and independent artisans who paid fees to practice their calling). The members of the upper house or Senate were to be, and to be elected by, the wealthier landowners, who also elected a governor for a term of three years. This person had authority as commander-in-chief of the militia, but his powers of appointment and veto were severely limited by two specially devised councils. The first, the Council of Appointment (proposed by Jay) was made up of the governor and one senator

[23] George Dangerfield, *Chancellor Robert R. Livingston of New York, 1746–1813* (New York: Harcourt, Brace and World, 1960), p. 88, and Spaulding, *op. cit.*, IV, 156–157.

[24] Monaghan, *op. cit.* pp. 94–95.

[25] *Journals of the Provincial Congress*, I, 842.

[26] *Spaulding (op. cit.*, pp. 158–166) discusses the completed document at great length and his analysis forms the primary basis for the following comments on the constitution.

chosen annually by the Assembly from each of the four senatorial districts and was responsible for most state appointments; only if the governor had a majority of supporters in the Assembly could he be in control of these appointments. The second, the Council of Revision (proposed by Livingston) was composed of the governor, the chancellor (the judge in charge of one of the major courts of the state), and the justices of the Supreme Court and had the right to veto bills within ten days of receiving them, but was subject to overrule by a two-thirds vote of both houses of the legislature. If the governor had support of the judges, he could control the veto, this was not easily accomplished, however, since the judiciary was built on the colonial system of a supreme court and lesser courts and was made independent by the provision that, upon good behavior, judges should hold office until the age of sixty.

Although the governor's power was weakened by the role of the two councils, the executive was not without authority. New York was one of the three states (Massachusetts and New Hampshire were the others) that applied the doctrine of separation of powers. In most states all-powerful legislatures dominated the governments and governors, but New York was less radical than most, and in her constitution the legislature was only one of the three separate branches of government.

The restrictions on the franchise (or right to vote), the creation of a bicameral or two-house legislature, the re-creation of the office of governor (although limited in power), his long term of three years, the establishment of an independent judiciary, the lack of a bill of rights, the absence of a provision for submitting the document to a popular vote—all cast the constitution in a conservative image, yet it was accepted by the Convention with only one dissenting vote, cast by Peter Livingston (an Albany merchant and Jay's uncle by marriage), who found it dangerously radical.[27] With the majority of people in the state favoring annual election, no property qualification for voting or holding office, and a strong popular legislature, how was such a constitution acceptable? The question cannot be answered simply for many complex factors seem to pertain: (1) the perilous situation in the state in regard to British forces; (2) the ballot form of voting; (3) the document, which had no formal bill of rights, but included several clauses that, grouped together, formed an unofficial one;[28] (4) the active role that the conservatives had played in the defense

[27] Dangerfield, *op. cit.,* pp. 92–93.
[28] The entire Declaration of Independence was included; the first article declared "that no authority shall upon any pretense whatever, be exercised over the people or members of this State but such as shall be derived from and granted by them"; article thirteen stated "that no member of this State shall be disfranchised or deprived of any rights or privileges secured to the subjects of this State by this constitution, unless by the law of the land, or the judgment of his peers."

of the state, thus establishing their loyalty and integrity beyond question; and (5) the fact that the conservative forces were well-organized and had produced an instrument that was compact and well written, reflected compromise, and was not seriously out of harmony with accepted political theory, in other words there were limitations on the governor and a reasonable balance of power among the executive, legislative, and judicial branches. Perhaps Robert Troup summed up best when he wrote to his friend Jay " . . . it preserves a proper Line between Aristocracy on the one Hand, and Democracy on the other.[29]

[READING NO. 11]

JAY'S VIEWS ON THE NEW STATE CONSTITUTION

Jay himself was not present when the Convention adopted the new constitution for New York State, nor for almost three weeks afterward, because of the death of his mother. Although he was responsible for much of it, he was critical of the final document, and two provisions that were added in his absence troubled him in particular. He wrote a strong letter to Livingston and Gouverneur Morris denouncing the clauses that allowed courts to appoint their own clerks and to license their own attorneys. Appointment of clerks by judges was ill-advised because:

The chancellor, and the judges of the Supreme Court holding permanent commissions, will be *tempted* not only to give those appointments to their children, brothers, relations, and favourites, but to continue them in office against the public good. You, I dare say, know men of too little probity, abilities, and industry to fill an office well, and yet of sufficient art and attention to avoid such gross misbehaviour as might justify loud clamours against them.

Besides, men who appoint others to offices, generally have a partiality for them, and are often disposed, on principles of pride as well as interest, to support them.

By the clerks of court being dependent on the judges collusion becomes more easy to be practised, and more difficult to be detected, and instead of publishing and punishing each other's transgressions, will combine in concealing, palliating, or excusing these mutual defects or misdemeanours.[30]

[29] Cited in Monaghan, *op. cit.,* p. 97.
[30] Jay, *Correspondence and Papers,* I, 132–132. April 29, 1777.

Jay regarded the provision for licensing attorneys as especially ill-conceived:

The new claims respecting the licensing of attorney, to speak plain, is in my opinion the most whimsical, crude and indigested thing I have met with.

There will be now between thirty and forty courts in this State, and, as that clause now stands, an attorney (however well qualified and licensed by the Supreme Court) must, before he can issue a writ in a little borough or mayor's court, obtain their license also. The reasons assigned for this seem to be: that it would be improper for one court to do this drudgery for the rest; that it would be difficult to distinguish which court it would be most proper to impose it upon; that the judges of the inferior courts might be offended at being relieved from this drudgery, thinking themselves as capable of judging of the merits of an attorney as of a cause, and that they had equal right with others to say who shall and who shall not be entitled to practise.

To say that it would be improper for one to do this drudgery for the rest, is begging the question. Other courts than the Supreme Court *never* had this drudgery to do; and I believe never will have in any part of the world, except in the State and by the Constitution of New York. Why the examination and licensing of attorneys should with more propriety be styled *a drudgery* than striking a jury, or any other business incident to the office of judge, I know not. If it be, I should think it ought not to be multiplied by thirty or forty, and then imposed on all in the State, compelling them to solicit and pay fees for admission to thirty or forty courts when one would have sufficed. . . .

The Supreme Court controls all the courts in the State which proceed according to the course of the common law, and its jurisdiction is bounded only by the limits of the State. An attorney is an officer of a common-law court. That court, therefore, which, by the Constitution, is made superior to the others, must be supposed most competent, not only to the determination of causes, but of the qualification of the attorneys who manage them.

The lesser courts cannot be deemed equally qualified for either; and being dependent and inferior in every other respect, ought not to have concurrent, independent, or equal authority in this. Justice as well as decency forbids that a mayor and four aldermen should constitutionally have a right to refuse admission to attorneys licensed by the Supreme Court.[31]

In the same letter Jay approved the other parts of the constitution, but regretted, "that like a harvest but before it was all ripe, some of the grains have shrunk . . ." and despite its defects, he would support it: "Though the birth of the Constitution is, in my opinon, premature, I shall nevertheless do all in my power to nurse and keep it alive, being far from approving the Spartan law which encouraged parents to destroy such of their children as perhaps by some cross accident might come into the world misshapen."

Jay regretted that the issue of slavery had not been met. During the debate on the constitution he had left the Convention on the very day that Gouverneur Morris proposed the abolition of slavery. The suggestion was favorably received, but it did not appear in the final document.[32] Had Jay been present and supported Morris' proposal, it might have carried. He made his position clear, as he wrote in the same letter to Livingston and Morris, "I should also have been for a clause against the continuation of domestic slavery."[33]

Despite Jay's reservations, the constitution was favorably received. William Duer, a wealthy New York merchant and banker, who was a member of Congress, wrote to him from the Second Continental Congress:

I congratulate you on the completion of the task of forming and organizing our new Government. I think it upon the maturest reflection the best system which has yet been adopted, and possibly as good as the temper of the times would admit. . . .[34]

The new system, "as good as the temper of the times would admit," was obviously workable, for it carried New York through the Revolution and the critical post-war period and later gave the men at the Constitutional Convention food for thought. Despite the cumbersome Councils of Appointment and Revision, this system of government existed with little

[31] *Ibid.,* pp. 132–134.

[32] Slavery continued in New York for many years although Jay's support as governor resulted in the passage by the legislature in 1799 of a law calling for the gradual abolition of slavery in the state (Monaghan, *op. cit.,* pp. 95–96, 411, 422).

[33] Jay, *Correspondence and Papers,* I, 136. Later, while in Europe (September 17, 1780), he wrote even more strongly to his friend Egbert Benson, "Were I in your legislature, I would prepare a bill for the purpose [abolition of slavery] with great care, and I would never cease moving it till it became a law or I ceased to be a member" (*ibid.,* p. 407). Upon his return to this country Jay helped to organize and became first president of the New York Society for Promoting the Manumission of Slaves.

[34] *Ibid.,* p. 138.

change for almost forty-five years or until a new constitutional convention convened in 1822.

A prominent American historian summed it up well when he wrote many years later, "Nowhere was a Constitution adopted under more difficult circumstances than in New York and nowhere was a better one written until Massachusetts performed the task in 1780. . . . At the time, and with reason, it was widely regarded as the best of the organic laws, and it exerted a considerable influence upon the Federal Constitution."[35]

The new state government was to go into effect on July 1, 1777, but a governor was not elected until July nor a legislature chosen until early September. To provide for a continuance of government until the meeting of the new legislature, the Convention appointed a Council of Safety with full powers to administer the affairs of the state — a move of vital necessity at a time when the British were attacking the northern part of the state and controlled most of the southern area. Before dissolving itself in favor of the new council, the Convention elected Livingston to be Chancellor and Jay to be Chief-Justice of the Supreme Court; both men narrowly defeated John Morin Scott, the ardent democrat.

[READING NO. 12]

JAY'S REFUSAL OF THE GOVERNORSHIP OF NEW YORK

Not much is known about the specifics of the election for the governorship. There was no campaign in the modern sense, but three candidates seemed to emerge: Philip J. Schuyler, a great land holder (or patroon) in upper New York, represented the conservative interests; John Morin Scott, the New York City radical; and George Clinton who, although a radical patriot, appealed to those of varied convictions, and was generally considered to be moderate.[36] Jay's contribution to his state had not gone unnoticed, and he too was regarded as a likely candidate, but he declined. In a letter to Abraham Yates in May of 1777 he made his position clear:

[Since] it would be proposed to hold me up as a candidate for the office of governor, I think it necessary to be very explicit on that subject. That the office of first magistrate of this State will be more respectable, as well as more lucrative, and consequently more desirable than the place I now fill, is very apparent. But, sir, my object in the course

[35] Allan Nevins, *The American States during and after the American Revolution, 1775–1789* (New York: The Macmillan Co., 1924), 158–161.

[36] Clinton had been a delegate to the Second Continental Congress and was serving as a brigadier general in the Continental Army.

of the present great contest neither has been, nor will be, either rank or money. I am persuaded that I can be more useful to the State in the office I now hold than in the one alluded to, and therefore think it my duty to continue in it.[37]

Later, four days prior to the election, in a letter to Leonard Gansevoort, a member of the New York convention, he stated again that he did not wish to run, and threw his support to Schuyler.

In my opinion I can be more useful in the place I now hold; and therefore, though the other is far more respectable as well as lucrative, yet, sir, the regard due to the public good induces me to decline this promotion.

I thought it necessary that you and others should be informed of my sentiments on this subject; and it would give me pleasure to hear that the electors in Albany had united in a design of voting for some one gentleman whose spirit, abilities, and reputation might recommend him to that important office. . . .

For my own part, I know of no person at present whom I would prefer to General Schuyler.[38]

The details of the election are only fragmentary. Whether General George Clinton drew both radical and conservative support or whether he received a majority of the soldier vote is not clear,[39] but he became the state's first governor. The election of this country lawyer, who did not have great land holdings, mercantile interests, or aristocratic family connections, was a keen disappointment to many conservatives, but they would make the best of the situation. Schuyler wrote to Jay in July:

I hope Gen. Clinton's having the chair of Government will not cause any divisions amongst the friends of America. Altho' his family and connections do not entitle him to so distinguished a predominance; yet he is virtuous and loves his country, has abilities and is brave, and hope he will experience from every patriot what I am resolved he shall have from me, support, countenance and comfort.[40]

---

[37] Jay, *Correspondence and Papers*, I, 136–137.

[38] *Ibid.*, p. 140–141.

[39] Spaulding *(op. cit.,* pp. 168–169) points out that Clinton had varied appeal to all groups, but that the decision to give qualified soldiers the right to vote was urged by Clinton's brother-in-law and may have been a key factor. Monaghan cites the soldier vote as decisive (Monaghan, *op. cit.,* p. 99).

[40] Jay, *Correspondence and Papers*, I, 147.

Despite their misgivings, the conservatives felt that the personal qualities of Clinton would enable him to lead his state, and in fact he was a strong and resolute wartime governor. What they did not anticipate was that Clinton would remain in office until the late 1780's and that, with a cooperative legislature, his forces were to frustrate, continually, conservative attempts to create more national power. Conservatives had written the constitution, but radicals would control the state.

[READING NO. 13]

THE PROMISE OF THE NEW CONSTITUTION: JAY'S ADDRESS

In September, 1777, the Supreme Court opened its first session at Kingston, and Chief Justice John Jay delivered an address to the grand jury of Ulster County. In his charge Jay capsuled the history of the conflict with England and echoed the determination of the people to win and maintain their freedom. Then he turned to the new constitution, and in words that stirred his audience he declared that:

. . . the highest respect has been paid to those great and equal rights of human nature, which should forever remain inviolate in every society, and that such care has been taken in the disposition of the legislative, executive, and judicial powers of government, as to promise permanence to the constitution, and give energy and impartiality to the distribution of justice. So that while you possess wisdom to discern and virtue to appoint men of worth and abilities to fill the offices of the State, you will be happy at home and respectable abroad. Your lives, your liberties, your property, will be at the disposal only of your Creator and yourselves. You will know no power but such as you will create; no authority unless derived from your grant; no laws but such as acquire all their obligation from your consent. . . .

Every man is permitted to consider, to adore, and to worship his Creator in the manner most agreeable to his conscience. No opinions are dictated, no rules of faith perscribed, no preference given to one sect to the prejudice of others. . . .

But let it be remembered that whatever marks of wisdom, experience, and patriotism there may be in your constitution, yet like the beautiful symmetry, the just proportion, and elegant forms of our first parents before their Maker breathed into them the breath of life, it is yet to be animated, and till then may indeed excite admiration, but will be of no use: from the people it must receive its spirit and by them be quickened. Let virtue, honour, the love of liberty and of science be and remain the soul of this constitution, and it will become the source of great and extensive happiness to this and future generations. Vice, ignorance, and want of vigilance will be the only enemies able to destroy it. Against these be forever jealous. Every member of the State ought diligently to read and to study the constitution of his country, and teach the rising generation to be free. By knowing their rights, they will sooner perceive when they are violated, and be the better prepared to defend and assert them.

This, gentlemen, is the first court held under the authority of our constitution, and I hope its proceedings will be such as to merit the approbation of the friends, and avoid giving cause of censure to the enemies of the present establishment.

It is proper to observe that no person in this State, however exalted or low his rank, however dignified or humble his station, but has a right to the protection of, and is amenable to, the laws of the land; and if those laws be wisely made and duly executed, innocence will be defended, oppression punished and vice restrained. Hence it become the common duty, and indeed the common interest of those concerned in the distribution of justice, to unite in repressing the licentious, in supporting the laws, and thereby diffusing the blessings of peace, security, order and good government, through all degrees and ranks of men among us.

I presume it will be unnecessary to remind you that neither fear, favour, resentment, or other personal and partial considerations should influence your conduct. Calm, deliberate, reason, candour, moderation, a dispassionate and yet a determined resolution to do your duty, will, I am persuaded, be the principles by which you will be directed.[41]

Jay's charge has been called one of the legal classics of the Revolution; the jury itself was so impressed that it requested that the address be published.[42]

[READING NO. 14]

PROBLEMS OF THE NEW SUPREME COURT

The Supreme Court had authority over only that part of the state controlled by the patriots; the richer area to the south remained under the

[41] Jay, *Correspondence and Papers*, I, 162–164.
[42] *Ibid.*, p. 158.

control of the old Supreme Court of the Province, a situation that in effect limited the new court's jurisdiction. As there are no published reports on the decisions of the new Supreme Court, it is difficult to assess Jay's role. In letters that he wrote in the spring and summer of 1778 we see that at least part of the time his duties concerned the growing lawlessness that existed in the state. To Gouverneur Morris in August of 1778 he wrote:

I am now engaged in the most disagreeable part of my duty, trying criminals. They multiply exceedingly. Robberies become frequent: the woods afford them shelter, and the tories food. Punishments must of course become certain, and mercy dormant—a rash system, repugnant to my feelings, but nevertheless necessary. In such circumstances lenity would be cruelty, and severity is found on the side of humanity.[43]

Three months later in a letter to his wife he wrote that conditions were still difficult and that firmness must be maintained:

. . . the number of persons charged with capital offenses, now in Confinement requires that Courts for their Tryal be speedily held—Delays in punishing Crimes encourages the Commission of them. The more certain & speedy the Punishment, the fewer will be the objects.[44]

[READING NO. 15]
CITIZENS' RIGHTS VS. MILITARY NECESSITY

Even during so critical a time, however, as pressure mounted for total support of the patriot cause, Jay firmly opposed illegal activities in the name of that cause. Military impressment of horses, teams, and carriages —without the intervention of a civil magistrate—was particularly offensive. When such actions were brought to his attention, he drew up a paper, entitled "A Hint to the Legislature of New York," in which he clearly and firmly opposed such an extraordinary exertion of power and urged the legislature to limit it:

It is the undoubted Right & an unalienable Privilege of a Freeman not to be divested, or interrupted in the innocent use, of Life, Liberty, or Property, but by Laws to which he has assented, either personally or by his Representatives. This is the Corner Stone of every free Con-

---

[43] *Ibid.*, p. 179.
[44] Letter to Sarah Jay cited in Monaghan, *op. cit.*, p. 102.

stitution, and to defend it from the Iron Hand of the Tyrant of Britain, all America is now in Arms; every Man in America being most deeply interested in its Preservation. Violations of this inestimable Right, by the King of Great Britain, or by an American Quarter Master, are of the same Nature, equally partaking of Injustice, and differing only in the Degree & Continuance of the Injury.[45]

[READING NO. 16]

VIOLATION OF CITIZENS' RIGHTS BY THE LEGISLATURE

In 1778 the split in state politics was growing more pronounced. The legislature was in the control of the small farmers and tradesmen, and Governor Clinton was using their support to further the war effort by passing legislation that seriously restricted the rights of the people. Livingston wrote to Schuyler that the legislature was "daily committing the most flagrant acts of injustice,"[46] and to Gouverneur Morris that "the Legislature has taken [measures] to banish money and monied men from the state."[47]

As Chief Justice, Jay sat on the Council of Revision, whose purpose was to provide a check upon "laws inconsistent with the spirit of this constitution or with the public good." Jay took this responsibility seriously and stood strongly against legislation that abused personal rights. Of the six bills that were vetoed by the council in 1778, five were rejected on the advice of Jay.[48]

One bill rejected by the council was designed to disfranchise and disqualify for office any person who had, since New York's ratification of independence in July of 1776, recognized the sovereignty of Great Britain or denied the authority of the new government. Jay argued that the legislature had neither existence nor authority prior to the adoption of the State constitution in April of 1777, and therefore could not legislate on acts committed before that time. He pointed out that the purpose of the resentful legislature was revenge, which was inconsistent "with the dignity or good of a free people."[49] Powerful as was Jay's reasoning, the temper of the times was such that the legislature overrode the veto.

Jay also objected to a bill to levy extra taxes on war profiteers:

[45] Iselin MSS, cited in Monaghan, *op. cit.,* p. 102.
[46] Dangerfield, *op. cit.,* p. 107.
[47] *Ibid.,* p. 108.
[48] Alfred Street, *The Council of Revision of the State of New York* (Albany, 1859), pp. 201–219. Cited in Monaghan, *op. cit.,* pp. 103–104. These excerpts are valuable in examining Jay's concept of law and government.
[49] Monaghan, *op. cit.,* p. 103.

No citizen is liable to be punished by the State, but such as have violated the laws of the State. . . . Supposing, therefore, that the persons *aimed* at in this bill have acquired their riches immorally, yet if they have acquired them in a manner which the Legislature has not thought proper to prohibit, they are not obnoxious to human punishment, however much they may be to divine vengeance. . . . [But if] those persons have acquired riches in a manner prohibited by the law of the land, they ought to be tried and punished in ways directed by these laws, and not subjected to double punishment.[50]

Jay's logic was overwhelming; this time the legislature did not override.

Jay's Return to the Philadelphia Congress

During the summer of 1778, the old Vermont controversy flared again.[51] New York and New Hampshire had for many years disputed this territory between them. When the king had ruled in favor of New York in 1764, many farmers, who held land grants from New Hampshire, were threatened with loss of their lands. Armed conflict seemed imminent, but the Revolution broke out, and New York's attention was diverted to meet the British invasion. In 1777 Vermont took advantage of the situation, declared herself an independent state, and drew up a constitution.

New York refused to renounce her claim, and now Massachusetts demanded the southern part of the disputed territory; everyone looked to Congress for a solution. New York was determined to send a man of considerable influence to represent her interests. Jay, a strong choice, accepted the assignment and left for Philadelphia in December of 1778.

Jay's work as a founder of the new State of New York was ended. Responsibilities in establishing the new nation occupied him until he returned in 1795 to be Governor of New York. In 1779 he resigned his position as Chief Justice of the state and was elected President of the Second Continental Congress.

[50] *Ibid.,* pp. 103–104.
[51] Discussed in detail in John Bell, "The Secession of Vermont," in Flick, ed., *The History of the State of New York,* V, 3–26.

CHAPTER IV

A Leader of the Confederation

When Jay returned to Philadelphia in early December, 1778, he was immediately thrust into political turmoil. In 1776, Congress had sent Silas Deane, Arthur Lee, and Benjamin Franklin to France to secure money and supplies for the war with Britain. The three commissioners had negotiated a treaty of alliance with France early in 1778. In July, 1778, Deane had been recalled for alleged corrupt dealings,[1] from which he had been unable to clear himself, and the situation continued to be embarrassing. Congress attempted to resolve the impasse by tabling the issue, and the matter dragged on without solution.

Deane, however, expected complete exoneration, and when, after months of waiting, he did not get it, he published an appeal "to the Free and Virtuous Citizens of America." It appeared on December 5, 1778, the day of Jay's arrival in Philadelphia, and it was a bombshell. In his own defense Deane indicted the conduct of his fellow commissioner, Arthur Lee,[2] brother of Richard Henry Lee, and virtually challenged the authority of Congress.[3] With support from Samuel Adams, who led an anti-French faction, Lee opposed Deane, while the supporters of Benjamin Franklin, one of the other commissioners in France, came to Deane's defense.

Jay was aware of the controversy, for he had been informed earlier while he was still in New York by both Gouverneur Morris and Robert Morris, that Deane, despite worthwhile contributions in France, was ill-treated by Congress.[4] At that time, he had taken no stand on the issue and

---

[1] A balanced account of this episode is contained in Richard Morris, *The Peacemakers: The Great Powers and American Independence* (New York: Harper & Row, 1965), pp. 8–13.

[2] Monaghan highlights Deane's charges against Lee, which he regards as legitimate (*John Jay: Defender of Liberty.* New York: The Bobbs-Merrill Company, 1935, pp. 110–111.)

[3] Page Smith, *John Adams* (Garden City: Doubleday, 1962. 2 vols.) I, 423–424. Smith emphasizes the attack on Congress, which he regards as threatening their integrity.

[4] Manuscript letters from late summer of 1778, cited Monaghan, *op. cit.*, p. 111.

the apparent intrigue behind it. Now, although Jay was not involved in the factional struggle, past experience dictated his course of action. He had helped secure Deane's appointment and regarded him as honest and patriotic; he had little regard for the Lees since his dispute with Richard Henry Lee in the previous Congress; he knew that the Lee–Adams faction was responsible for General Schuyler's loss of public favor.[5] He must support Deane.

President of the Continental Congress

The seething political cauldron bubbled over when Henry Laurens, President of the Second Continental Congress, attempted to have Congress censure Deane's publication, which he deemed offensive. When Laurens could not muster enough votes, he resigned his office, on December 9, 1778. The following day, despite attempts to return Laurens to the chair, the majority of the delegates favored a New Yorker, and Jay was persuaded to accept the post.[6]

RELATIONS WITH FRANCE

However, Jay's election did not calm the seething waters. In an earlier visit to Philadelphia, Washington had sensed that there were too many self-interests in Congress:

Idleness, dissipation and extravagance seem to have laid fast hold of most [members]. That Speculation, peculation, and an insatiable thirst for riches seems to have gotten the better of every other consideration and almost every order of Men. That party disputes and personal quarrels are the great business of the day.[7]

Arthur Lee had secured the services of Thomas Paine, secretary to the Committee for Foreign Affairs, who not only revived the charges against

[5] Philip J. Schuyler of New York was replaced as commander of the northern armies by General Horatio Gates. Jay and Schuyler exchanged several letters on the matter, and as late as March, 1779, Jay notified Schuyler that Congress had refused to accept the latter's resignation from service, even though the delegates from "New England and Pennsylvania [are] against you . . . the commander-in-chief wishes you to retain your commission." Schuyler was heartsick and soon retired from public life. John Jay, *Correspondence and Public Papers of John Jay,* ed. Henry P. Johnson (New York: G. P. Putnam's Sons, 1890–1893. 4 vols.), I, 193–194.
[6] *Journals of the Continental Congress, 1774–1789,* ed. Worthington C. Ford and Gaillard Hunt (Washington, D.C.: United States Government Printing Office, 1904–1937. 34 vols.), XII, 1203–1206.
[7] George Washington, *The Writings of George Washington,* ed. John C. Fitzpatrick (Washington, D.C.: United States Government Printing Office, 1931–1940. 39 vols.), XIII, 467. December 30, 1778.

Deane, but in a correlated attack on Robert Morris, who was raising funds to carry on the war,[8] indiscreetly revealed the extent of secret French aid given to America prior to the Alliance.[9] Recognizing the embarrassment to the French, who had been giving contrary assurances to England, Congress censured Paine and voted to remove him from his post.[10]

Several months earlier, Jay had expressed some doubts about the French treaty. In a letter to Robert R. Livingston he had written "If Britain would acknowledge our independence, and enter into a liberal alliance with us, I should prefer a connexion with her to a league with any power on earth."[11] But, by early 1779, England had not granted independence, and now Jay viewed the French treaty as vital to his own country's interest. He assured Gérard, the French Minister to America, that he supported the Alliance and the prestige of his office was behind it.[12]

MILITARY PROBLEMS

Meanwhile Jay, as President of Congress, had to deal with a threat to General Washington's command of the Continental Army.

[READING NO. 17]
A LETTER TO REASSURE GENERAL WASHINGTON

During the spring of 1779, Washington wrote Jay of his concern with the conduct of General Horatio Gates, who seemed to be attempting to discredit the Commander-in-Chief in order to win favor in the eyes of Congress.[13] Earlier Rutledge had warned Jay that a cabal had formed against Washington that was "more injurious to the well-being of the continent than the sword of Sir Harry [Clinton] and his whole army."[14]

Jay, in a warm letter to Washington that undoubtedly cemented a firm relationship between the two men that continued all their lives, reassured the General of the support of Congress. The arrows of ingratitude and dishonor would strike hard in the perilous times ahead, but a better day was coming:

[8] Morris demanded that Congress investigate his conduct and accounts. Jay, as President of Congress, wrote to him of his vindication. "It gives me great pleasure to transmit to you an unanimous act of Congress . . . not only acquitting your conduct in the transaction it relates to of blame, but giving it . . . express approbation . . ." (Jay, *Correspondence and Papers*, I, 188).

[9] Morris, *op. cit.*, p. 10.

[10] *Journals of the Continental Congress*, XIII, 75. January 8, 1779.

[11] Jay, *Correspondence and Papers*, I, 180. April 29, 1778.

[12] Monaghan, *op. cit.*, p. 113.

[13] Jay, *Correspondence and Papers*, I, 204.

[14] *Ibid.*, p. 184. Sir Henry Clinton replaced Sir William Howe as commander of the British forces in America on May 8, 1778.

I value the esteem and regard of the wise and virtuous; and had wished to know the particulars of transactions respecting which only vague and unsatisfactory reports had come to my knowledge. Delicacy forbade my breaking the subject to you when here. I was sure of your politeness, but not certain of more than a usual degree of confidence. The latter has now become manifest, and permit me to assure you it shall be mutual. The impression attempted to be made has not taken. It passed without a single remark. Your friends thought it merited nothing but silence and neglect. The same reason induced me to take no notice of it in my answer.

I have perused the several papers with which you favoured me. The delicacy, candour, and temper diffused through your letters form a strong contrast to the evasions and design observable in some others. Gratitude ought to have attached a certain gentleman to the friend who raised him; a spurious ambition, however, has, it seems, made him your enemy. This is not uncommon. To the dishonour of human nature, the history of mankind has many pages filled with similar instances; and we have little reason to expect that the annals of the present or future times will present us with fewer characters of this class. On the contrary, there is reason to expect that they will multiply in the course of this revolution. Seasons of general heat, tumult, and fermentation favour the production and growth of some great virtues, and of many great and little vices. Which will predominate, is a question which events not yet produced nor now to be discerned can alone determine. What parties and factions will arise, to what objects be directed, what sacrifices they will require, and who will be the victims, are matters beyond the sphere of human prescience. New modes of government, not generally understood, nor in certain instances approved—want of moderation and information in the people—want of abilities and rectitude in some of their rulers—a wide field open for the operations of ambition—men raised from low degrees to high stations, and rendered giddy by elevation and the extent of their views—a revolution in private property and in national attachments—laws dictated by the spirit of the times, not the spirit of justice and liberal policy—latitude in principles as well as commerce—suspension of education—fluctuations in manners, and public counsels, and moral obligations—indifference to religion, etc., etc., are circumstances that portend evils which much prudence, vigour, and circumspection are necessary to prevent or control. To me, there appears reason to expect a long storm and difficult navigation. Calm repose and the sweets of undisturbed retirement appear more distant than a peace with Britain. It gives me pleasure, however, to reflect that the period is approaching when we shall become citizens of a better-ordered state; and the spending a few troublesome years of our eternity in doing good to this and future generations is not to be avoided nor regretted. Things will come right, and these States will be great and flourishing. The dissolution of our government threw us into a political chaos. Time, wisdom, and perseverance will reduce it into form, and give it strength, order, and harmony. In this work you are, to speak in the style of one of your professions, a master-builder; and God grant that you may long continue a *free* and *accepted* mason.[15]

Washington, of course, continued in command, although his leadership was challenged again on later occasions.

One of Jay's responsibilities as President of Congress was to ensure the wise use of limited American military strength. The following letter to General LaFayette illustrates his cool judgment.

[READING NO. 18]

AGAINST LAFAYETTE'S PROPOSED INVASION OF CANADA

LaFayette had earlier proposed an invasion of Canada, a grandiose scheme for liberating the French people of the area. While it received some support in Congress, it was firmly opposed by Washington, who regarded it as contrary to the best interest of his country for the French to control this territory.[16] Washington's strong opposition convinced Jay that the plan was not feasible, and he wrote to LaFayette of the decision of Congress to shelve it.

Prudence therefore dictates that the arms of America should be employed in expelling the enemy from her own shores before the liberation of a neighbouring province is undertaken, as the proportion of force necessary for our defence must be determined by the future operations and designs of the enemy, which cannot now be known; and as, in case of another campaign, it may happen to be very inconvenient if not impossible for us to furnish our proposed quota of troops for the

---

[15] *Ibid*, pp. 04–206.

[16] Washington, *Writings*, XIV, 378–383. April 14, 1779.

emancipation of Canada. Congress think they ought not, under such circumstances, to draw their good ally into a measure the issue of which, depending on a variety of contingencies, is very uncertain, and might be very ruinous.[17]

PAPER MONEY AND PUBLIC CREDIT

Jay and Congress faced few more serious problems than those of raising money, curbing the issue of paper money that quickly became almost worthless, and maintaining the credit of Congress.

[READING NO. 19]
JAY'S LETTER TO THE STATES AGAINST PAPER MONEY

Acutely aware of the serious condition of American Currency, Jay wrote to Washington in April, 1779: "The state of our currency is really serious. Where or by what means the progress of the depreciation will be prevented is uncertain."[18] In July he was informed by his friend, Egbert Benson: "Taxation is the only *honest* and rational recovery for the depreciation of the Currency, but I fear it will be too slow in its operation to answer the present purpose and recourse must be had to other expedients."[19] By September, Congress was concerned enough to request that Jay draw up a circular letter to the states to accompany a copy of their resolutions for stopping the further emissions of bills of credit. Jay's draft deplored the artificial depreciation of the currency, analyzing as the cause the mistrust of the people in the ability and inclinations of America to honor its bills; but reassuring those same people, he called for renewed confidence and effort. The words were sharp, the language clear:

The artificial depreciation . . . merits minute investigation. A distrust, however occasioned, entertained by the mass of the people, either in the ability or inclination of the United States, to redeem their bills, is the cause of it. Let us inquire how far reason will justify a distrust in the ability of the United States.

The ability of the United States must depend upon two things: first, the success of the present revolution; and, secondly, on the sufficiency of the natural wealth, value, and resources of the country.

[17] Jay, *Correspondence and Papers*, I, 186. January 3, 1779.

[18] *Ibid.*, p. 210. April 26, 1779.

[19] *Ibid.*, p. 214. July 6, 1779. Egbert Benson was a New York lawyer and legislator during the Revolution; he remained a close friend of Jay throughout his life.

61

That the time has been when honest men might, without being chargeable with timidity, have doubted the success of the present revolution, we admit; but that period is passed. The independence of America is now as fixed as fate, and the petulant efforts of Britain to break it down are. as vain and fruitless as the raging of the waves which beat against her cliffs. . . .

In close alliance with one of the most powerful nations in Europe, which has generously made our cause her own, in amity with many others, and enjoying the good-will of all, what danger have we to fear from Britain? Instead of acquiring accessions of territory by conquest, the limits of her empire daily contract; her fleets no longer rule the ocean, nor are her armies invincible by land. How many of her standards, wrested from the hands of her champions, are among your trophies, and have graced the triumphs of your troops? And how great is the number of those who, sent to bind you in fetters, have become your captives, and received their lives at your hands? In short, whoever considers that these States are daily increasing in power; that their armies have become veteran; that their governments, founded in freedoom, are established; that their fertile country and their affectionate ally furnish them with ample supplies; that the Spanish monarch, well prepared for war, with fleets and armies ready for combat, and a treasury overflowing with wealth, has entered the lists against Britain; that the other European nations, often insulted by her pride, and alarmed at the strides of her ambition, have left her to her fate; that Ireland, wearied with her oppressions, is panting for liberty; and even Scotland displeased and uneasy at her edicts;—whoever considers these things, instead of doubting the issue of the war, will rejoice in the glorious, the sure, and certain prospect of success. This point being established, the next question is, whether the natural wealth, value, and resources of the country will be equal to the payment of the debt. . . .

It is well known that the inhabitants of this country increased almost in the ratio of compound interest. By natural population they doubled every twenty years; and how great may be the host of emigrants from other countries, cannot be ascertained. . . . Thus, you see, great part of your debt will be payable, not merely by the present number of inhabitants, but by that number swelled and increased by the natural population of the present inhabitants, by multitudes of emigrants [sic] daily arriving from other countries, and by the natural population of those successive emigrants, so that every person's share of the debt will be constantly diminishing by others coming to pay a proportion of it. . . .

No country will produce more people than it can subsist; and every country, if free and cultivated, will produce as many as it can maintain. Hence we may form some idea of the future population of these States. Extensive wilderness, now scarcely known or explored, remain yet to be cultivated, and vast lakes and rivers, whose waters have for ages rolled in silence and obscurity to the ocean, are yet to hear the din of industry, become subservient to commerce, and boast delightful villas, gilded spires, and spacious cities rising on their banks. . . .

Having shown that there is no reason to doubt the ability of the United States to pay their debt, let us next inquire whether as much can be said for their inclination. . . .

The enemy, aware that the strength of America lay in the union of her citizens and the wisdom and integrity of those to whom they committed the direction of their affairs, have taken unwearied pains to disunite and alarm the people, to depreciate the abilities and virtue of their rulers, and to impair the confidence reposed in them by their constituents. To this end, repeated attempts have been made to draw an absurd and fanciful line of distinction between the Congress and the people, and to create an opinion and a belief that their interests and views were different and opposed. Hence the ridiculous tales, the invidious insinuations, and the whimsical suspicions that have been forged and propagated by disguised emissaries and traitors in the garb of patriots. Hence has proceeded the notable discovery, that as the Congress made the money they also can destroy it, and that it will exist no longer than they find it convenient to permit it. . . . It certainly cannot be necessary to remind you, that . . . it is no more in their power to annihilate your money than your independence, and that any act of theirs for either of those purposes would be null and void. . . .

A bankrupt, faithless republic would be a novelty in the political world, and appear among reputable nations like a common prostitute among chaste and respectable matrons. The pride of America revolts from the idea; her citizens know for what purpose these emissions were made, and have repeatedly plighted their faith for the redemption of them; they are to be found in every man's possession, and every man is interested in their being redeemed; they must therefore entertain a high opinion of American credulity who suppose the people capable of believing, on due reflection, that all America will, against the faith, the honour, and the interest of all America, be ever prevailed upon to countenance, support, or permit so ruinous, so disgraceful a measure. . . .

If, then, neither our ability nor inclination to discharge the public debt is justly questionable, let our conduct correspond with this confidence, and let us rescue our credit from its present imputations. . . .

It has been already observed, that in order to prevent the further natural depreciation of our bills, we have resolved to stop the press, and to call upon you for supplies by loans and taxes. You are in capacity to afford them, and are bound by the strongest ties to do it. . . . Recollect that it is the price of the liberty, the peace, and the safety of yourselves and poserity that now is required; that peace, liberty, and safety, for the attainment and security of which you have so often and so solemnly declared your readiness to sacrifice your lives and fortunes. . . . Provide, therefore, for continuing your armies in the field till victory and peace shall lead them home; and avoid the reproach of permitting the currency to depreciate in your hands when, by yielding a part of taxes and loans, the whole might have been appreciated and preserved. Humanity as well as justice makes this demand upon you. . . . Rouse, therefore; strive who shall do most for his country; rekindle that flame of patriotism which, at the mention of disgrace and slavery, blazed throughout America and animated all her citizens. Determine to finish the contest as you began it, honestly and gloriously. Let it never be said, that America had no sooner become independent than she became insolvent, or that her infant glories and growing fame were obscured and tarnished by broken contracts and violated faith, in the very hour when all the nations of the earth were admiring and almost adoring the splendour of her rising.[20]

Congress, impressed with Jay's efforts, unanimously approved the draft and once again ordered a special German translation.[21]

American Relations with France and Spain

Jay served as President of Congress for less than a year. In the autumn of 1779, Congress appointed him Minister to Spain, and for the next fifteen years Jay was concerned with American foreign relations and diplomacy.

[20] Jay, *Correspondence and Papers*, I, 218–236. September 13, 1779.
[21] Years later it also was translated and published in Paris in an effort to curb the issuance of paper money during the French Revolution (Monaghan, *op. cit.*, p. 122).

In accepting an alliance with the new American states in 1778, the French had been generous: they promised and gave financial, naval, and military aid, and pledged to continue the war until American independence should be established. The French also promised not to keep any part of America that their forces might conquer. Perhaps France hoped that gratitude would tie the United States to France, and increase the influence of France both in America and Europe.[22]

France, however, was not prepared or able to pay for full scale war, and in order to avoid defeat abroad and the financial disaster at home that years of extravagance by the French court seemed to portend, France sought desperately to draw Spain into the war. Charles Gravier, Comte de Vergennes, French Foreign Minister, sought to convince the Conde de Floridablanca, his counterpart in Madrid, that the two nations had a mutual interest in a British defeat.

[READING NO. 20]
JAY'S TERMS FOR A TREATY WITH SPAIN

Spain was not overjoyed at the prospect of aiding and abetting a rebellion that might set a bad example for her own colonies in the new world; therefore Floridablanca demanded Florida, full control of the Mississippi River for Spain, and repossession of Canada for France, obviously hoping to contain the new nation between territory controlled by the two European powers. [23] In order to meet those excessive demands, Vergennes needed the assurance of Congress that the American states would go along. Gérard, the French envoy, visited Jay frequently in Philadelphia to secure his support but the President of Congress was wary. Later, he recorded his modifications of Gérard's demands:

It was therefore my opinion that we sho[u]ld quit all claim to the Floridas & grant them the navigation on their River below our Territory on their giving us a convenient free part of it under Regulations to be specified in a Treaty, provided they w[oul]d acknowledge our Independence, defend with their arms, and grant us either a proper Sum of Money or an annual Subsidy for a certain Numb. of Years. Such then was the situation of things as to induce me to think that a Conduct so decided and spirited on the part of Spain w[oul]d speedily bring about a Peace and that Great Britain, rather than hazard the

---

[22] *The American Secretaries of State and Their Diplomacy*, ed. Samuel Flagg Bemis (New York: The Pageant Book Co., 1958. 10 vols.), I, 289–293 contains a copy of the alliance.

[23] Morris, *op. cit.*, pp. 14–17.

Loss of Canada, Nova Scotia . . . by cont[inuin]g the War w[oul]d
yield the Floridas to Spain & Independence to us.[24]

Gérard, concerned with the rumors of impending peace talks between
the United States and England, had secured from Congress in January,
1779, the declaration that "these United States will not consider either
truce or peace with the common enemy, without the formal consent of
their ally [France] first obtained."[25] Now he kept the pressure on the congress to accept Spanish conditions, which were in conflict with American
peace proposals.[26] For several months Congress debated its committee's
recommendations and Gérard's demands. The old suspicion and divsion
within Congress were revived and once again the French Alliance seemed
in jeopardy. However, in August, the Chevalier Luzerne replaced Gérard
and brought news that Spain had entered the war against England.
Renewed enthusiasm for the Alliance swept over Congress, which now
decided to elect an official envoy to Spain. The embers of the Lee–Deane
controversy, however, still smoldered. The supporters of Arthur Lee nominated him for the new post, and, at the same time, hoped to elect John
Adams as peace commissioner to negotiate treaties when the war should
end. Adams was proposed first for the latter post, but the Deane adherents
countered by nominating Jay. When neither Adams nor Jay could obtain
a majority, a compromise was struck: Jay was nominated and elected
minister plenipotentiary to Spain, defeating Arthur Lee, and Adams then
was chosen unanimously as peace commissioner.[27]

Gérard was elated with Jay's choice for the Spanish post. He wrote to
Vergennes: "To much intelligence and the best intentions he joins an
amiable and conciliatory temper."[28] He seemed to misinterpret Jay's
friendliness and cordiality for pliability. Time was soon to prove that
Gérard had misjudged his man. Both in Madrid and later in Paris Jay was
a firm and determinated negotiator, who frustrated the attempts of France
and Spain to limit the political independence of his country.[29]

[24] John Jay, unfinished manuscript of his Spanish mission cited in Monaghan, *op. cit.,*
pp. 120–121.
[25] *Journals of the Continental Congress,* XIII, 63.
[26] In February, a committee recommended among other conditions that this country
have free navigation of the Mississippi River to the Southern boundary of the United
States and free commerce to a port or ports below that boundary (*Journals of the
Continental Congress,* XIII, 239–244).
[27] *Journals of the Continental Congress,* XV, 1113. September 27, 1779. The details of
the election are discussed in Morris, *op. cit.,* pp. 12–13.
[28] Cited in Morris, *op. cit.,* p. 16.
[29] Jay did not know at the time he was appointed that France, as a part of her alliance
with Spain, had agreed not to make peace without Spanish consent and to continue
the war until Gibraltar was obtained, thereby enlarging the war without America's
consent or even knowledge (Morris, *op. cit.,* p. 16).

CHAPTER V

A Founder of an
Independent Nation

Jay must have accepted his post as Minister Plenipotentiary to Spain with some reluctance. He was permitted by the state constitution to hold the office of Chief Justice of New York and to represent the state in Congress at the same time, and he had done so for several months. But in August, 1779, he had resigned as Chief Justice, and during that same month he hinted to Governor Clinton that he might retire from Congress:

Popularity is not among the number of my objects; a seat in Congress I do not desire, and as ambition has in no instance drawn me into public life, I am sure it will never influence me to continue in it. Were I to consult my interest I should settle here and make a fortune; were I guided by inclination I should now be attending to a family who, independent of other misfortunes, have suffered severely in the present contest.[1]

Despite his yearning to leave the political turmoil, he could not reject this new opportunity to serve his country in Europe, and he began to wind up his affairs in Congress. The high regard in which Jay was held can be seen in letters that he received from Washington and Edward Pendleton, the Virginia lawyer and delegate, in early October, 1779. Washington pointed hopefully to the future:

Permit me, amongst the number of your friends to congratulate you and my Country, on your late honourable, and important appointment. be assured Sir

---

[1] John Jay, *Correspondence and Public Papers of John Jay*, ed. Henry P. Johnson (New York: G. P. Putnam's Sons, 1890–1893. 4 vols.), I, 217. August 27, 1779.

that my pleasure on this occasion though it may be equalled, cann[o]t be exceeded by that of any other.

I do most sincerely wish you a pleasant and agreeable passage. The most perfect and honourable accomplishment of your ministry, and a safe return to the bosom of a grateful Country.[2]

Pendleton reflected on the past:

I congratulate you, sir, upon your appointment to represent the American States at the court of Madrid; the just testimony of that confidence which the honourable body you have presided over, have in your abilities and integrity. May health, success, and every felicity accompany you; but, while I am sensible of the advantages we shall reap from your eminent services there, I have my fears that they will be missed, importantly, where you now are; and that the spirit of party, almost laid to sleep, will revive upon your absence. . . .[3]

Jay knew that his Spanish assignment would pose difficulties, writing to Washington, he seemed to have few illusions:

Among the objects of my mission are some which, however just, will not be easily attained, and therefore its success will be precarious, and probably partial. The only satisfaction I promise myself from this appointment, will flow from the rectitude with which the duties of it will be discharged, and not from a prospect of general approbation.[4]

However, neither Jay nor anyone else could foresee the immense obstacles that would continually thwart his mission, which included: (1) the recognition of the United States as an independent country, (2) the procurement of financial aid, and (3) the negotiation of a treaty with Spain. Not only would he face the diplomatic skills of the formidable Floridablanca in Madrid and the determined maneuvers of Vergennes in Paris, but because of the congressional appointment of William Carmichael to be secretary to the mission, and Jay's personal selection of his brother-in-law, Brockholst Livingston, as his personal secretary, he was continually surrounded by duplicity in his official family.

Jay had written to Washington several months earlier about the manipu-

---

[2] George Washington, *The Writings of George Washington*, ed. John C. Fitzpatrick (Washington, D.C.: United States Government Printing Office, 1931–1944. 39 vols.) XVI, 425.

[3] Jay, *Correspondence and Papers*, I, 247. October 11, 1779.

[4] *Ibid.*, p. 248. October 14, 1779.

lations of Congress, "There is . . . much intrigue in this Statehouse,"[5] but the events in Europe would make his days in Congress seem uneventual by comparison. During his stay abroad servants, aides, spies, counterspies, agents, double agents, ministers with and without portfolio, envoys, special envoys, kings, queens, emperors, empresses, and various and sundry others would attempt to block American independence. None of them succeeded in doing so, however, and that Congress, through ignorance and bungling, did not inadvertently destroy the American cause was in a large sense due to Jay's tireless efforts.

[READING NO. 21]

JAY'S RECEPTION IN SPAIN

When Jay landed at Cadiz in Spain in late January, 1780, he found the political climate chilly. While waiting several weeks for his official acceptance by the Spanish court, he had a strong hint that his difficulties were just beginning. King Charles III refused officially to receive Gérard, who had accompanied Jay from America as retiring French Minister to the United States, for to do so might imply recognition of the independence of America.[6] Finally, in early March, Jay heard from the Conde de Floridablanca, and the Spanish Foreign Minister's communiqué made it clear that the American's acceptance by the court must not be in an official capacity.

. . . his Majesty highly approves the choice, which the American Congress have made of you to the trust mentioned in your letter, as well on account of the high estimation in which his Majesty holds the members who made the choice, as the information he has received of your probity, talents, and abilities.

His Majesty also received with pleasure the information of the desire which the Colonies have to form a connexion with Spain, of whose good disposition they have already received strong proofs. Nevertheless, his Majesty thinks it necessary in the first place, that the manner, the forms, and the mutual correspondence should be settled, upon which the Union must be founded, which the United States of America desire to establish with this monarchy . . . there is no obstacle to your Excellency's coming to this Court, in order to explain your intentions and those of the Congress, and to hear those of his Majesty, and by that means settling a basis upon which a perfect friendship may be established, and also its extent and consequences.

[5] *Ibid.*, p. 210. April 26, 1779.
[6] Richard Morris, *The Peacemakers: The Great Powers and American Independence* (New York: Harper & Row, 1965), p. 45.

His Majesty thinks, that until these points are settled, as he hopes they will be, it is not proper for your Excellency to assume a formal character, which must depend on a public acknowledgment and future treaty.[7]

Although he prepared to leave for Madrid, Jay reacted strongly to the obvious slight to his nation. His irritation was clear in the report he sent to Congress:

. . . the acknowledgment of [independence] is not to be made because we are independent, which would be candid and liberal, but because of the previous considerations we are to give for it, which is consistent with the principles on which nations usually act. . . . it would, in my opinion, be better for America to have no treaty with Spain than to purchase one on such servile terms. There was a time when it might have been proper to have given that country something for their making common cause with us, but that day is now past. Spain is at war with Britain.[8]

Jay had no way of knowing Floridablanca's real intentions for America, but the latter had discussed them with the French envoy to Spain, Comte de Montmorin, who sent word to the Comte de Vergennes, the French Foreign Minister, that Floridablanca was pressing for the thirteen states to be designated feudal dependencies of England, a status designed to create quarrels between Britain and America, which Spain and France could exploit to their mutual advantage.[9] Vergennes, however, continued to urge acceptance of American independence as a way to swing the balance of power in Europe away from England and toward France.[10]

On his arrival in Madrid, Jay received Floridablanca's letter demanding specific information relating to "the civil and military state of the American Provinces, and of their resources to continue the present war, not only for the defense of their own liberty, but also with respect to the aid and succors that they may be able to afford Spain in its operations, in case hereafter this Crown should become the ally of America."[11]

Jay's reply suggested that what Floridablanca wanted "if fully answered, would produce a very interesting history of the present condition of the

[7] Jay, *Correspondence and Papers,* I, 273. March 3, 1780.

[8] *Ibid.,* pp. 274–275. March 3, 1780.

[9] Montmorin's letter to Vergennes is cited in Morris, *op. cit.,* p. 45.

[10] Morris, *op. cit.,* p. 47.

[11] Jay, *Correspondence and Papers,* I, 278.

American States."[12] Nevertheless, he detailed the determination of the United States to win its full independence and outlined the obvious advantages to Spain to provide supplies and money to aid the American cause.[13] Despite its indisputable logic, Jay's letter was ignored by Floridablanca, thus continuing the pattern of frustration that was to last throughout the American's stay in Spain.

Financial Problems

In late April, Jay received a letter from the Committee of Foreign Affairs informing him that in November, Congress had passed resolves drawing bills upon him of one hundred thousand pounds, or about five hundred thousand dollars, payable in six months.[14] With less than one month left before the bills were due, Jay had not yet met with Floridablanca. The situation demanded immediate action, and Jay sent an urgent note to the Spanish Minister, explaining the bills and requesting that the matter be called to the attention of the king.[15]

Floridablanca could no longer deny the American an audience and met with Jay in early May. Skillfully avoiding any commitment on the bills—although he hinted that an advance by the end of the year was possible—Floridablanca chose to emphasize the king's firmness in maintaining exclusive navigation rights to the Mississippi.[16]

[READING NO. 22]
JAY'S FINANCIAL EMBARRASSMENT

Jay realized that, as the envoy of a new nation engaged in a desperate struggle for its survival and encountering great financial difficulties in the process, his funds would be limited, but his position was becoming precarious. It pained him to report to Congress in May:

The credit given by Congress to Dr. Franklin is expended, and I am without other means of obtaining supplies than by private credit, which I am at a loss to satisfy. To apply to, and be maintained by the

---

[12] *Ibid.*, p. 280.

[13] For a full reply see *ibid.*, pp. 280–303.

[14] *Jay Papers* cited in Morris, *op. cit.*, p. 50. Congress, in desperate financial straits, had borrowed the money from creditors who were to be repaid from funds that Jay was to request from the Spanish government; since there was no guarantee that Spain would grant the loan, Jay was left in an untenable situation.

[15] Jay, *Correspondence and Papers*, I, 311–314.

[16] Jay's notes on this conference can be found in *ibid.*, pp. 316–324.

Court, is, in my opinion, too humiliating for the public good; and as
yet I have neither received nor heard of remittances from America. It
would give me pleasure to know in what manner Congress mean I
should be supplied, and whether any measures have been taken for
that purpose. . . . The salary allowed me, so far from admitting the
expense of private couriers, is inadequate for the common purposes
for which it was given. This is a delicate subject, and I wish it was
not my duty to say anything respecting it. This place is the dearest in
Europe. The Court is never stationary, passing part of the year in no
less than five places . . . Madrid, Pardo, Aranjues, St. Ildefonso, and
the Escurial, hence considerable expenses arise. I forebear enumerating
particulars, my design being only to mention this matter to Congress,
not to press it upon them. I shall always live agreeably to my circumstances; and if, from their being too narrow, inconveniences result to
the public, they ought to be informed of it. I hope what I have said
will be viewed in this light only; so far as I am personally interested,
I am content.[17]

His conference with Floridablanca, while continuing the Spanish game
of doubletalk and delay, did nourish one hopeful prospect for Jay—
negotiation on a personal level. However, it now raised a question of
ethics for him; should he discuss the meeting with Montmorin in order
to keep the French envoy informed of Jay's progress? He put the question
squarely to Floridablanca. Was the conference "either in the whole or in
part . . . confidential?"[18] The dilemma was resolved when Floridablanca
responded "you may [discuss] it freely."[19]

The exchange highlighted a fundamental difference between the American minister and his European counterpart. To Jay, acting with duplicity
was immoral and therefore intolerable no matter what the immediate advantages, but to Floridablanca it was not a matter of morality at all, but a
fact of diplomacy that was often the key to successful negotiations. Had
he felt it essential to keep the details of the conference from Montmorin
he would not have hesitated to do so, but since he often discussed Spanish
policy toward America with the French diplomat, it was not necessary.
John Adams seemed to sense that Floridablanca represented a different
political and diplomatic world, although he was unable adequately to
explain it. He wrote to Jay in May:

[17] *Ibid.*, pp. 338–339.
[18] *Ibid.*, p. 326.
[19] *Ibid.*, p. 327.

. . . there is something in the European understanding different from that we have been more used to. Men of the greatest abilities, and the most experience are with great difficulty brought to see, what appears to us as clear as day. It is habit, it is education, prejudice, what you will, but so it is.[20]

And so it was. Floridablanca used this "European understanding" as a powerful weapon to thwart the success of Jay's mission.

Clear evidence of Floridablanca's duplicity was apparent in his dealing with two English agents in Spain, Thomas Hussey and Richard Cumberland. The former, who was a priest, was also a paid member of a Spanish spy ring, and thus was serving as a double agent; the latter, a playwright, was a social climber who was friendly with high English politicians; together they formed a team to seek an accommodation between England and Spain. To Floridablanca this meant England's withdrawal from Gibraltar in exchange for Spain's making peace, but which the English interpreted as the giving up of West Florida in return for Spain's agreement to sever military and trade relations with the United States.[21] Neither nation would concede the other's demands, but for months Floridablanca hopefully, if fruitlessly, kept negotiations alive. In the midst of this intrigue it is not difficult to understand why he had little inclination to treat seriously with the minister from America.[22] When Jay—noticing the intimacy with which Hussey and Cumberland were received by the royal court in contrast to the cool treatment that he had received—questioned the possibility that these two men were working in the British interest, Floridablanca calmly assured him that Hussey was in Spain due to the death of an uncle and Cumberland was only passing through on his way to Italy; and to divert Jay's mind, he hinted at the King's intention of expressing some "tangible" evidence of his feeling for the Americans.[23]

[READING NO. 23]
JAY'S INDIGNATION

Despite Floridablanca's assurances, the Spanish government made no funds available to guarantee the bills that Congress had drawn upon Jay. When they began to appear in Spain, Jay's position became increasingly difficult; where possible he deferred payment, but unless the bills were

[20] *Ibid.,* p. 330.
[21] This strange and unsuccessful mission is documented in detail in Morris, *op. cit.,* pp. 51–65.
[22] Floridablanca's correspondence with Hussey reveals that he played up Jay's presence in a vain attempt to speed up the unofficial negotiations with the British (*ibid.,* p. 54).
[23] *Ibid.,* p. 225.

honored in a reasonable time, the creditors would be entitled to damages and interest. In a letter to Floridablanca in June, he pointed out:

the anxiety and painful concern with which Congress would receive intelligence of the failure of their bills, and especially after the expectations they have been induced to conceive of the successful issue of their affairs here. What conclusions would draw from the inability of Spain to advance the sum in question, even to men actually in arms against Great Britain, I forbear to mention, nor would it become me to point out the several evil consequences flowing from such an event, to those who enjoy from nature and experience more discernment than I am blessed with. I still flatter myself that some expedients may be devised to surmount the present difficulties and that the harvest of laurels now ripening for his Majesty in America will not be permitted to wither for want of watering. . . .[24]

When Floridablanca, by late August, still offered no assistance, Jay decided to present his case to Montmorin, who advised him to beseech Floridablanca for another meeting. Jay was in no mood to beg, and his notes reveal the following conversation:

. . . he [Montmorin] would by all means advise me to write the Minister another letter, praying an audience. I answered that the object of my coming to Spain was to make *propositions* not *supplications*, and that I should forbear troubling the Minister with further letters, till he should be more disposed to attend to them. That I considered America as being, and to continue, independent in *fact*, and that her becoming so in *name* was of no further importance than as it concerned the common cause, in the success of which all the parties were interested; and that I did not imagine Congress would agree to purchase from Spain the acknowledgment of an undeniable fact at the price she demanded for it; that I intended to abide patiently the fate of the bills, and should transmit to Congress an account of all matters relative to them; that I should then write the Minister another letter on the subject of the treaty, and if that should be treated with like neglect, or if I should be informed that his Catholic Majesty declined going into that measure, I should then consider my business at an end,

[24] Jay, *Correspondence and Papers*, I, 355. June 9, 1780.

and proceed to take the necessary measures for returning to America.[25]

Montmorin could do little to improve Jay's rapport with Floridablanca, but he did transmit the request for financial assistance to the French government.[26]

[READING NO. 24]
JAY'S PROPOSED COURIER SYSTEM

Not only were the bills still hanging like the sword of Damocles and the treaty negotiations stalled, but secret instructions from Congress were of little value to Jay. It took months to receive official correspondence, some of which was already outdated before it was delivered through normal diplomatic channels, but to make matters worse this correspondence usually was opened by the Spanish and, despite the use of different ciphers, was readily decoded.[27] As a result, the Spanish seemed always forewarned, and Jay was at a severe disadvantage in his dealings with Floridablanca. In late November Jay wrote to Congress proposing a special courier system.

I must request your attention to the necessity of putting your correspondence with the public servants in Europe on a better footing. I am now at the expense of sending Colonel [Brockholst] Livingston to the seaside with my despatches, with orders to wait for American vessels, and deliver them to the captain with his own hands. I receive no letters by the post, but with marks of inspection, and after much delay.

Some that I write never come to hand, and I know of letters having arrived from America for me, which I have never seen, and never expect to see. . . . I cannot even find a courier that I can depend on. Is it not time for America, like other nations, to provide against these inconveniences by proper regulations and establishments? Would it not be well to have American agents or consuls in one or more of the

---

[25] *Ibid.,* pp. 389–390.

[26] Although Spain did eventually guarantee $150,000, only help from Franklin, the French government, and private banking sources saved some of the bills from being protested and prevented large penalties from being invoked, which obviously would not only have been a great source of personal embarrassment to Jay, but a grievous blow to the credit of his government *(ibid.,* pp. 442–444).

[27] Unknown to Congress at the time, Luzerne, who had replaced Gérard as the French envoy to the United States, and others in his legation obtained the key to all important diplomatic ciphers used by American diplomats in Europe; these were delivered to Vergennes, who in turn made them available to the Spanish (Morris, *op. cit.,* p. 211).

ports of France and Spain? Public despatches might be sent by packet-boats, or other vessels, to these agents, and should on no account be delivered to any other person; the agents might be ordered to send them to the Courts to which they may be directed by a trusty American—one of the officers of the ship, for example; and he should be ordered to wait for, and return with, the despatches of the Minister.

Would it not . . . be proper to provide for the safe-conduct of letters to Congress after their arrival in America? I have reason not only to suspect, but to believe, that certain persons in America are attentive to these matters, and care should be taken to keep American letters out of their way.

This is an important subject and merits attention. For my own part I find several persons here who have more intelligence from America than myself; and it is the more mortifying when considered that they are probably often indebted for their information to the contents of letters directed to me.[28]

But Congress took no action on his suggestion, and Jay continued to play against a stacked deck. When he realized that even personal mail was being opened, he commented in a letter in which he used several Spanish phrases that he hoped that they were accurate, but if not perhaps the Spanish postmaster would kindly correct them.[29]

Jay's personal problems must have added to his frustration. Neither he nor his wife was in robust health, and their little daughter died at three weeks of age. To add to his difficulties Sally's brother, Brockholst Livingston, made a habit of making rude and capricious remarks about Americans, Congress, and his own brother-in-law, which served to embarrass both his sister and her husband. At the same time he seemed to be sharing diplomatic secrets with William Carmichael, the secretary to the legation, whom Jay distrusted and refused to permit to copy his confidential reports to Congress.[30]

When Brockholst was due to leave for America, Mrs. Jay wrote a long letter to their father, explaining her brother's ungracious behavior. She mailed it to her sister Kitty to be given to her father only if Brockholst attempted to defame Jay.[31] Like her husband, she too, was suspicious of Carmichael, and in the same letter blamed him for her brother's conduct.

[28] Jay, *Correspondence and Papers,* I, 453–455.

[29] Cited in Monaghan, *op. cit.,* p. 152.

[30] Morris *op. cit.,* p. 236.

[31] Since Brockholst was captured by the British on his way home and on his final return remained silent about Jay, the letter was never delivered to Mrs. Jay's father.

My emotions are very great when I reflect upon the insidious & cruel manner in which Mr. Carmichael has treated Mr. Jay. . . . With this gentlemen the Col[one]l. [Brockholst] has form'd the strictest intimacy, swallowing unwarily all his artful baits . . . *he* has made Brockholst act a part so foreign to the welfare of himself & interest of the family. . . .[32]

Carmichael, who remained in charge of American affairs in Madrid after Jay left Spain, was an able public servant, but he was irritated by Jay's concern for protocol and felt that his superior was too self-righteous. At times he made decisions without consulting Jay; when the latter reminded him of the limits of his responsibilities, Carmichael resented the reproof.[33] While the two continued their official relationship for as long as Jay remained in Spain, the latter never forgot Carmichael's conduct. Years later, as he was going over his correspondence, Jay made the following notation on the Carmichael papers:

Care should be taken of these Papers. They include Letters to and from William Carmichael—a Man who mistook cunning for wisdom; and who in pursuing his Purposes, preferred the Guidance of artifice and Simulation, to that of Truth and Rectitude. He finally yielded to Intemperance, and died a Bankrupt.[34]

A further complication presented itself in the person of a young Virginian named Lewis Littlepage, whom Jay had agreed to supervise in Spain as a favor to his friend Thomas Adams, a Virginia delegate in Congress. While Jay supported him so he could be a student, he spent most of his time chasing women, seeking military glory, or conniving against Jay. After Jay refused to honor certain bills that Littlepage had run up and tried to collect payment on others, the youth followed Jay to Paris and futilely challenged him to a duel, and then to New York where he came out second best in a pamphlet attack on his benefactor.[35]

Under such trying circumstances a man less resolute than Jay might have packed his bags and returned home; certainly he was discouraged, but he refused to give in. To his wife Sally he was "virtue's own self," and she found him "composed in danger, resigned in affliction, and even

[32] Letter cited in Monaghan, *op. cit.*, p. 157.

[33] Morris, *op. cit.*, p. 237.

[34] Iselin MSS., cited in Monaghan, *op. cit.*, p. 159. For a more complete and less harsh account of William Carmichael, see Samuel G. Coe, *The Mission of William Carmichael to Spain* (Baltimore: Johns Hopkins University Press, 1928).

[35] Details of Jay's relationship with Brockholst Livingston, William Carmichael, and Lewis Littlepage are detailed in Monaghan, *op. cit.*, pp. 153–165, 223–224, 235–243.

possessing a cheerful disposition in every circumstance."[36] Had he known, however, the extent of French efforts to pressure Congress to accept the Spanish demands on the Mississippi question, thus further tying his hands, even Jay might have regarded his situation as beyond repair.

[READING NO. 25]
JAY'S RESERVATIONS ON THE MISSISSIPPI QUESTION

Luzerne had been working for months in Philadelphia to persuade Congress to relinquish American claims to the Mississippi,[37] which they finally agreed to do, and in February, 1781, Jay was ordered

to recede from the (earlier) instructions . . . so far as they insist on the free navigation of that part of the river Mississippi, which lies below the thirty-first degree of north latitude, and on a free port or ports below the same; provided such cession shall be unalterably insisted upon by Spain; and provided the free navigation of the said river, above the said degree of north latitude, shall be acknowledged and guarantied by his Catholic Majesty to the citizens of the United States in common with his own subjects.[38]

Jay did not know of the change in instructions until May and did not inform Floridablanca until July, but the Spanish were aware of this new directive before Jay officially presented it, a fact that supported his earlier request for a courier system and, in this instance, prevented him from forcing the Spanish Minister's hand. In a long report to Congress in October, Jay indicated his reservations on the whole matter of America's relationship with Spain. His report also shows how a skillful diplomat makes the best use of such strength as he commands.

My only difficulty arose from this single question: Whether I could prudently risk acting on a presumption, either that Spain did not already or would not soon be acquainted with the contents of this instruction. If such a presumption had been admissible, I should without the least hesitation, have played the game a little further, keeping this instruction in my hand as a trump card, to prevent a separate peace between Spain and Britain, in case such an event should otherwise prove inevitable. Had Spain been at peace with our ene-

[36] Letter of Sarah Livingston cited in Morris, *op. cit.,* p. 236.
[37] *Ibid.,* pp. 237–239.
[38] Jay, *Correspondence and Papers,* I, 461.

mies, and offered to acknowledge, guarantee, and fight for our independence, provided we would yield them this point (as once seemed to be the case), I should, for my own part, have no more hesitation about it now than I had then. But Spain being now at war with Great Britain, to gain her own objects, she doubtless will prosecute it full as vigorously as if she fought for our objects. There was and is little reason to suppose that such a cession would render her exertions more vigorous, or her aids to us much more liberal. The effect which an alliance between Spain and America would have on Britain and other nations would certainly be in our favour, but whether more so than the free navigation of the Mississippi is less certain. The cession of this navigation will, in my opinion, render a future war with Spain unavoidable, and I shall look upon my subscribing to the one as fixing the certainty of the other.

I say I should have played this game a little further, if the presumption before mentioned had been admissible, because it has uniformly been my opinion, that if after sending me here Congress had constantly avoided all questions about the Mississippi, and appeared to consider that point as irrevocable, Spain would have endeavoured to purchase it by money, or a free port, but as her hopes of a change in the opinion of Congress were excited and kept alive by successive accounts of debates and intended debates on that question, and as Congress by drawing bills without previous funds had painted their distress for want of money in very strong colors, Spain began to consider America as a petitioner, and treated her accordingly. But as by the intervention of Dr. Franklin our bills for near six months were safe, and as after this resolution of the 15th of February there was reason to expect that the subject of it would not soon be resumed in Congress, I should, in case I could have depended on this instruction being and remaining a secret, have thought it my duty to have given the United States a fair trial for the Mississippi, or at least for a free port near it. With this view I should have appeared to give myself no concern about the bills, applied for no aids, made no offers, and on all proper occasions have treated an alliance with Spain as an event which, though wished for by us, was not essential to our safety, and as the price demanded for it apppeared to us unreasonable, it was not probable we should agree. I think we should then have been courted in our turn. . . . But . . . the Ministry were well acquainted with the contents of this instruction. . . . The moment they saw that the cession of this navigation was made to depend on their persevering to insist upon it, it became absurd to suppose that they would cease to persevere.[39]

Jay's frustration had continued throughout the summer and fall of 1781. On the matter of the bills, Franklin had informed him in June:

If you are unable to pay them, they must be posted, for it will not be in my favor to help you. And I see nothing will cure Congress of this madness of drawing upon the Pump at Oldgate, but such a proof that its well has a bottom.[40]

Apparently the "well" was not quite empty, for Franklin found more credit in Paris, relieving Jay of some of the mounting pressure of the bills.

[READING NO. 26]
A PROPOSED TREATY WITH SPAIN

When Floridablanca requested in September that Jay submit a preliminary draft of a treaty between the United States and Spain, the American drew one up in a matter of days. In the proposed treaty Jay followed his new instructions, relinquishing to Spain the navigation of the Mississippi south of 31 degrees, but he still had reservations on the matter and felt it his duty to frankly declare:

that the difficulty of reconciling this measure to the feelings of their constituents has appeared to Congress in a serious light, and they now expect to do it only by placing in the opposite scale the gratitude due to his Catholic Majesty, and the great and various advantages which the United States will derive from the acknowledgment and generous support of their independence by the Spanish monarchy at a time when the vicissitudes, dangers, and difficulties of a distressing war with a powerful, obstinate, and vindictive nation renders the friendship and avowed protection of his Catholic Majesty in a very particular manner interesting to them. The offer of this proposition, therefore, being dictated by these expectations and this combination of circumstances, must necessarily be limited by them, and consequently that if the acceptance of it should, together with the proposed alliance, be postponed to a general peace, the United States will cease to con-

---

[39] *Ibid.*, II, 86–88. October 3, 1781.
[40] *Ibid.*, p. 40. June 30, 1781.

sider themselves bound by any proposition or offers which he may now make in their behalf.[41]

The clever Floridablanca ignored Jay's proposals, and in so doing he out-smarted himself. His judgment, warped by a fear of an independent America, caused him to reject a treaty that granted Spain its full claims on the Mississippi in return for recognition of a new nation whose existence could no longer be ignored. The failure of Spain to act must rank as an enormous diplomatic mistake; Jay's foresight in making the grant condi-tional kept American claims alive until finally recognized by Spain in 1795. Throughout the winter of 1781–1782, Floridablanca continued his policy of delay; news of the American victory at Yorktown arrived in December, but it had little effect. Until Jay left Madrid in May, 1782, he made no no further "progress" with the Spanish government. He was, however, to suffer a final indignity.

[READING NO. 27]

A DINNER INVITATION DECLINED

In March, 1782, Floridablanca sent a note with an official invitation to dine at his table every Saturday after the 11th of May. It was left at Jay's house, but not addressed to Jay personally. When the American discreetly inquired through Montmorin as to its authenticity, Floridablanca indicated that it was left in error, but that the king would permit Jay to attend "as a private gentlemen of distinction."[42] Jay doubted any mistake and refused to attend, as he wrote to Montmorin, because no

Minister or representative of an independent sovereign can with pro-priety accept an invitation which *in the terms of it,* impeaches his title to that character. . . . Whatever doubts this or other Courts may enter-tain relative to their independence, the United States entertain none, and therefore their servants ought not by word or action to admit any. . . . All arguments from the expediency [of accepting the invitation] must cease to operate . . . although particular circumstances may some-times render it expedient for a nation to make great sacrifices to the attainment of national objects, yet it can in no case be expedient for them to impair their honor, their dignity, or their independence.[43]

---

[41] *Ibid.,* pp. 125–126. September 22, 1781.
[42] Morris, *op. cit.,* p. 245.
[43] Cited in Monaghan, *op. cit.,* p. 178.

Appointment to the Paris Peace Commission

While Jay had been pursuing a hopeless course in Spain, many overtures were made to settle the war without consulting America. Catherine the Great of Russia, Maria Theresa, and later her son, Joseph II of Austria, Jacques Necker, Director General of Finance in France, and numerous others interjected themselves into the peace efforts.[44] These efforts were unsuccessful, although France had reached a decision to pressure the United States through Luzerne in Philadelphia to appoint new peace commissioners to modify John Adams' influence in any future negotiations.

When Congress chose a new peace commission, Jay, Franklin, Laurens, and Jefferson were elected with Adams, and were given instructions that left their decisions subject to the approval of the French government. Vergennes mistakenly thought that the obdurate New Englander's influence in future negotiations would be drastically limited.[45] But the French had overreached themselves and, as a result, suffered the consequences. The Americans bearing the heaviest responsibility on the commission were Adams and Jay. The normally suspicious New Englander was now thoroughly aroused and even less susceptible to French influence, while the normally sympathetic New Yorker was greatly disturbed by the humiliating instructions that went with his new commission and in time came thoroughly to distrust French intentions. In their actions at Philadelphia the French may well have snatched defeat from the jaws of victory.

[READING NO. 28]
JAY'S PROTEST AGAINST HIS INSTRUCTIONS

Gouverneur Morris wrote to Jay, offering condolences on his appointment:

when you come to find by your instructions that you must ultimately obey the dictates of the French minister, I am sure that there is something in your bosom which will revolt and the servility of the situation. . . . Do I not know you well enough to believe that you will not act in this new capacity? I think I do; and therefore I will express my concern that you must decline the honour, if that name can be applied to such offices.[46]

Morris correctly anticipated Jay's revulsion, but not his sense of duty. In a long letter to the President of Congress on September 20, 1781, Jay wrote:

---

[44] Their efforts are brilliantly and systematically detailed in Morris, op. cit., pp. 88–190.
[45] Jefferson never served, and Laurens was captured by the British on his way to Europe and only arrived at the end of the negotiations.
[46] Jay, Correspondence and Papers, II, 38–39.

The new commissions with which Congress have honoured me argue a degree of confidence which demands my warmest acknowledgments; and which, so far as it may be founded on an opinion of my zeal and integrity, they may be assured will not prove misplaced.

At the commencement of the present troubles I determined to devote myself, during the continuance of them, to the service of my country, in any station in which she might think it proper to place me. This resolution, for the first time, now embarrasses me. I know it to be my duty, as a public servant, to be guided by my own judgment only in matters referred to my discretion; and, in other cases, faithfully to execute my *instructions* without questioning the policy of them. But there is *one* among those which accompany the commissions, which occasions sensations I never before experienced, and induces me to wish my name had been omitted. So far as personal pride and reluctance to humiliation may render this appointment disagreeable, I view it as a very unimportant circumstance; and should Congress, on any occasion, think it for the public good to place me in a station inferior and subordinate to the one I now hold, they will find me ready to descend from the one, and cheerfully undertake the duties of the other. My ambition will always be more gratified in being useful than conspicuous; for in my opinion, the solid dignity of a man depends less on the height or extent of the sphere allotted to him, than on the manner in which he may fulfil the duties of it.

But, sir, as an American, I feel an interest in the dignity of my country, which renders it difficult for me to reconcile myself to the idea of the sovereign independent States of America, submitting, in the persons of their ministers, to be absolutely governed by the *advice* and *opinion* of the servants of another sovereign, especially in a case of such national importance.

That gratitude and confidence are due to our allies is not to be questioned; and that it will probably be in the power of France almost to dictate the terms of peace for us, is but too true. That such extraordinary extent of confidence *may* stimulate our allies to the highest efforts of a generous friendship in our favour, is not to be denied; and that *this instruction* receives some appearance of policy from this consideration, may be admitted. I must, nevertheless, take the liberty of observing, that however our situation may, in the opinion of Congress, render it necessary to relax their demands on every side, and even to direct their commissioners ultimately to concur (if nothing better can be

83

done) in any peace or truce not subversive of our independence, which France may be determined to accede to, yet that this instruction, besides breathing a degree of complacency not quite republican, puts it out of the power of your Ministers to improve those chances and opportunities which, in the course of human affairs, happen more or less frequently unto all men. Nor is it clear that America, thus casting herself into the arms of the King of France, will advance either her interest or reputation with that or other nations.

What the sentiments of my colleagues on this occasion may be, I do not as yet know; nor can I foresee how far the negotiations of the ensuing winter may call for the execution of this commission. Thus circumstanced, and at such a distance from America, it would not be proper to decline this appointment. I will, therefore, do my best endeavours to fulfil the expectations of Congress on this subject; but as, for my own part, I think it improbable that serious negotiations for peace will soon take place, I must entreat Congress to take an early opportunity of relieving me from a station where, in character of their Minister, I must necessarily receive and obey (under the name of *opinions*) the directions of those on whom I really think no American minister ought to be dependent, and to whom, in love for our country, and zeal for her service, I am sure that my colleagues and myself are at least equal.[47]

From Spain to Paris

Congress did not relieve him of the new commission, and when Richard Oswald appeared in Paris with unofficial peace feelers from the English government, Franklin requested the other commissioners to join him. He wrote to Jay in late April, 1782:

Here you are greatly wanted, for messingers begin to come and go, and there is much talk of a treaty proposed; but I can neither make, nor agree to propositions of peace, without the assistance of my colleagues. Mr. Adams, I am afraid, cannot just now leave Holland. Mr. Jefferson is not in Europe, and Mr. Laurens is a prisoner. . . . Render yourself here as soon as possible. You would be of infinite service. Spain has taken four years to consider whether she should treat with us or not. Give her forty, and let us in the meantime mind our own business.[48]

[47] *Ibid.,* pp. 70–72.
[48] *Ibid.,* p. 193.

Jay had been suffering a prolonged attack of rheumatism throughout the early months of 1782, to add to all the other aggravation of his stay in Spain. Personally, he had no reason not to go to Paris immediately, but his sense of duty prevailed, and he delayed his departure for several days until he was assured by Floridablanca that discussion on a treaty with Spain could continue through the Spanish envoy in France.[49]

Despite the fact that he had never been officially received by the Spanish Court, he had conducted himself with dignity and upheld the honor of his country at all times and although his mission in Spain was not successful, the lessons that he learned in diplomacy were invaluable. As he shook the Spanish dust from his boots in late May, 1782, he was ready for his new assignment. This time he knew what to expect; the Europeans would regret that they had been such good teachers.

Negotiating a Peace Treaty

Arriving in Paris the latter part of June, 1782, Jay hastened to consult with Franklin on the progress of negotiations.[50] When Jay contracted influenza a few days later, Franklin continued alone in the informal talks with Richard Oswald, now chief of the British commissioners.[51] In August Oswald received official confirmation of his status as peace commissioner and showed it to Jay, who was back on his feet, but the American took exception to the terms of the commission. Oswald recounted Jay's reaction:

By the quotation from the Act of Parliament in the Commission he supposed it was meant that Independence was to be treated upon: and was to be granted perhaps as the price of peace: that it ought to be no part of a Treaty: it ought to have been expressly granted by Act of Parliament, and an order for all troops to be withdrawn, previous to any proposal for Treaty: as that was not done, the King he said, ought to do it by Proclamation and order all garrisons to be evacuated, and then close the American war by treaty.[52]

[49] Floridablanca commented tersely to his envoy in France, the Conde de Aranda, about Jay's mission: "His two chief points were: Spain, recognize our independence; Spain, give us more money." Cited in Morris, *op. cit.,* p. 246.

[50] The struggle between Lord Shelburne, the Colonial Secretary, and Charles James Fox, the Foreign Secretary, for control of the British end of the negotiations, which resulted in a victory for Shelburne, is ably described in Morris, *op. cit.,* pp. 257–281.

[51] Franklin grouped his suggestions to Oswald into two categories, those that were *necessary:* independence, settlement of boundaries, confining Canada's boundaries to their pre-war limits, and Newfoundland fishing rights; and those that were *advisable,* the most important of which was the cession of Canada to the United States. Franklin's *necessary* terms formed the heart of the eventual treaty. *The American Secretaries of State and Their Diplomacy,* ed. Samuel Flagg Bemis (New York: The Pageant Book Co., 1958. 10 vols.), I, 60–61.

[52] Cited *ibid.,* p. 63.

Oswald was unsettled by Jay's position, and his letters to Lord Shelburne reveal that it helped convince him that more liberal concessions were necessary.[53]

[READING NO. 29]

A DECISION TO DISOBEY CONGRESS

Meanwhile, Jay had met with Conde de Aranda, Floridablanca's envoy to France, to continue negotiations for a mutual treaty; but the latter proposed a western boundary of the United States that was far short of the Mississippi River, and Jay would have none of it. He wrote: "Having thus clearly discovered the views of Spain, and that they were utterly inadmissible, I had little hope of our ever agreeing, especially as the Mississippi was, and ought to be our *ultimatum*."[54]

Jay, joined by Franklin, discussed the Spanish proposal with Vergennes and his secretary, Rayneval, and he was visibly disturbed by the French Minister's apparent support of Aranda: it now seemed clear that the French were playing the Spanish game. In a conversation with Franklin that evening, he made it clear that France could not be relied on: as it was in her interest to see us separated from England but not have us become a great and powerful nation, we must act on our own initiative. Franklin reminded Jay about the instructions that meant Vergennes had to be consulted and his advice accepted. Would he break those instructions? Smoking his long clay pipe, Jay listened thoughtfully to his colleague; his response was unmistakedly clear:

Unless we violate these instructions the dignity of Congress will be in the dust. . . . I do not mean that we should deviate in the least from our treaty with France. . . . Our honor and our interests are concerned in inviolably adhering to it, but if we lean on her love of liberty, her affections for Americans, or her interested magnanimity, we shall lean on a broken reed that will sooner or later pierce our hands. . . . If the instructions conflict with America's honor and dignity I would break them—like this.[55]

[53] Although Oswald discussed reasons for a new commission, these letters indicate that he was not opposed to Franklin's *advisable* terms of the cession of Canada; however the American commissioners did not exert any real pressure on this issue, and it was quietly dropped (*ibid.*, pp. 66–67).

[54] This passage is part of a long report on the negotiations that Jay wrote to Secretary for Foreign Affairs Livingston in November, 1782 (Jay, *Correspondence and Paper*, II, 391).

[55] This conversation, constructed from various Jay letters, is cited in Morris, *op. cit.*, p. 310.

With a deliberate motion he hurled his pipe into the fireplace where it shattered into many pieces.[56] Perhaps in that crucible the independence of the United States was hardened.

Late in August, Franklin became incapacitated, because of a kidney stone with complications of gout, leaving Jay in charge of the peace commission. His suspicions thoroughly aroused, Jay maintained a "hard line" in negotiations, supported strongly by Adams, who wrote from Holland:

For my own part I am not the minister of . . . any 'American Colonies.' . . . I think we ought not to treat at all until we see a minister authorized to treat with 'the United States' of America, or with their ministers. Our country will feel the miserable consequence of a different conduct if we are betrayed into negotiations . . . before this point is settled. . . . Firmness! and patience for a few months will carry us triumphantly to that point where it is in the interests of our allies, of neutral nations, nay, even of our enemies, that we should arrive. I mean a sovereignty universally acknowledged by all the world.[57]

In early September, talks with Rayneval, Vergennes' secretary, further convinced Jay that France was no longer interested in establishing American claims to the Mississippi and now might possibly decide to negotiate with England to restrict land claims in the Ohio valley.[58] When he received word that Rayneval had left secretly for England, he was convinced that the visit might endanger the American cause and he decided on the most daring step of his career. Without informing Vergennes or his own colleague, Franklin, and disregarding his official instructions, he sent a private emissary, Benjamin Vaughan, to inform the English that it was in their interests to cut the ties that bound America to the French by granting a change in Oswald's commission, thus giving him authority to treat with the ministers of the United States.[59] The gamble paid off, for in late September Oswald received his new commission, although not without some misgivings from Lord Shelburne. The latter wrote that

we have put the greatest confidence, I believe ever placed in men, in the American commissioners. It is now to be seen, how far they or America are to be depended upon. . . . There never was a greater risk run. I hope the public will be the gainer, else our heads must answer for it and deservedly.[60]

[56] The pipe breaking is described in Monaghan, *op. cit.*, p. 197.
[57] Jay, *Correspondence and Papers*, II, pp. 328–329.
[58] Discussed in Jay's report to Secretary Livingston (*ibid.*, pp. 398–399).
[59] Jay's instructions to Vaughan are found *ibid.*, pp. 403–407. He had modified his stand from independence as a previous condition to a treaty to Adams' suggestion that the British commissioners be empowered to treat with the United States of America.
[60] Shelburne's letter to Oswald is cited in Monaghan, *op. cit.*, p. 205.

Jay then drafted treaty proposals, which Franklin approved but which were not communicated to Vergennes: they included full independence, withdrawal of British troops, a share in the Newfoundland fisheries, free navigation of the Mississippi River, and reciprocal trade concessions between Great Britain and the United States, and the settlement of boundary disputes.[61] Oswald transmitted the proposals to London, but as a result of British military success at Gibraltar, they were not favorably received.

In late October John Adams arrived in Paris in response to Jay's urgent call. When informed of the progress of negotiations, he mistakenly believed that a rift had grown between Franklin and Jay, and he did not trust the doctor. He wrote in his diary:

Between two as subtle Spirits as any in this World, the one malicious, the other I think honest, I shall have a delicate, a nice, a critical part to Act. F.s cunning will be to divide us. To this End he will provoke, he will insinuate, he will intrigue, he will maneuvre. My Curiosity will at least be employed in observing his Invention and his Artifice. J. declares roundly, that he will never set his hand to a bad Peace. Congress may appoint another, but he will make a good Peace or none.[62]

A few days later Franklin was visited by Adams, who recorded his own comments:

I told him [Franklin] without Reserve my Opinion of the Policy of this Court and of the Principles, Wisdom and Firmness with which Mr. Jay had conducted the Negotiation in his Sickness and my Absence, and that I was determined to support Mr. Jay to the utmost of my Power.[63]

Franklin listened in silence; he later resolved that, whatever his personal feeling, the American commissioners must present a united front, and he communicated nothing to the French court until the preliminary negotiations were completed.

On October 29, 1782, the American and British negotiators met.[64] The English countered Jay's original proposals with others: modifying boundary claims, setting restrictions on the fisheries, demanding satisfaction for

---

[61] The proposals were an elaboration on Franklin's earlier "necessary articles" (*The American Secretaries of State*, I, 75).

[62] Adams, *Diary and Autobiography*, III, 38–39. October 27, 1782.

[63] *Ibid.*, p. 82.

[64] Laurens, the fourth American commissioner, arrived for the final day of negotiations; the fifth, Jefferson, never left the United States. Oswald had been joined earlier by Shelburne's secretary, Henry Strachey, and a young career diplomat, Alleyne Fitzherbert.

Loyalists and for British creditors, and claiming lands in the Ohio region and in the province of Maine. For one month the negotiators haggled over terms. Finally on November 29, they settled the two major disputed issues—the fishing rights and Loyalist claims—setting the stage for the official signing the next day.[65] While these were only preliminary articles and a final treaty could not be approved for many months, the American commissioners—by ignoring their instructions—had made independence a reality.

Two formidable jobs remained, however: to justify the conduct of the Americans to Vergennes and to their own Congress. The United States needed another French loan desperately and could not indulge in the luxury of ignoring the feelings of Vergennes, who was distressed at the turn of events. To the amiable Franklin fell the responsibility of handling Vergennes, and his letter explaining American action was masterfully written. He admitted that

We have been guilty of neglecting a point of *bienséance* [propriety]. But as this was not from want of respect for the King, whom we all love and honour, we hope it will be excused, and that the great work, which has hitherto been so happily conducted, is so nearly brought to perfection, and is so glorious to his reign, will not be ruined by a single indiscretion of ours. Certainly the whole edifice sinks to the ground immediately, if you refuse on that account to give us assistance. . . . The English, I just now learn flatter themselves they have already divided us. I hope this little misunderstanding will therefore be kept secret, and they will find themselves totally mistaken.[66]

Whether it was Franklin's logic or his charm, Vergennes seemed convinced, and he wrote to Luzerne that he could not blame anyone, including Franklin, and authorized another large loan to the United States.

[READING NO. 30]
JAY'S DEFENSE OF A CRUCIAL DECISION

The task of informing Congress of the actions of the commissioners fell to Jay.

---

[65] On the disputed issues, the British accepted American demands for fishing rights, while the Americans agreed to *recommend* that the Loyalist claims be honored *(ibid.,* pp. 92–95).

[66] *The Revolutionary Diplomatic Correspondence of the United States,* ed. Francis Wharton (Washington, D.C.: United States Government Printing Office, 1889. 6 vols.), VI, 143–144.

As we had reason to imagine that [certain] articles . . . did not correspond with the policy of the Court, we did not communicate the preliminaries to the Minister until after they were signed.[67]

Later Congress debated the commissioners' propriety in accepting the treaty without consulting the French. It was a delicate matter, yet a treaty had been signed with obvious advantages, which caused genuine rejoicing. Neither a motion to censure nor one to commend could carry, and Congress adjourned without doing either.[68] However, the Secretary for Foreign Affairs, Robert R. Livingston, without authorization from Congress, wrote a rebuke to the commissioners, declaring that their secrecy was unwarranted.[69] The criticism stung Jay and he responded:

Your doubts respecting the propriety of our conduct in that instance appear to have arisen from the following circumstances, viz.:

1st. That we entertained and were influenced by distrusts and suspicions which do not seem to you to have been altogether well founded.

2d. That we signed the articles without previously communicating them to this Court.

With respect to the first. In our negotiations with the British commissioner, it was essential to insist on, and, if possible, obtain, his consent to four important concessions.

1st. That Britain should treat with us as being what we were, viz., an independent people. The French Minister thought this demand premature, and that it ought to arise from, and not precede, the treaty.

2d. That Britain should agree to the extent of boundary we claimed. The French Minister thought our demands on that head extravagant in themselves, and as militating against certain views of Spain which he was disposed to favour.

3d. That Britain should admit our right in common to the fishery. The French Minister thought this demand too extensive.

4th. That Britain should not insist on our reinstating the tories. The French Minister argued that they ought to be reinstated.

Was it unnatural for us to conclude from these facts that the French Minister was opposed to our succeeding on these four great points, in

[67] *Ibid.*, p. 133.

[68] The discussion in Congress is detailed in Morris, *op. cit.*, pp. 442–443.

[69] *Revolutionary Diplomatic Correspondence*, VI, 338–340. March 25, 1783.

the extent we wished? It appeared evident that his plan of a treaty for America was far from being such as America would have preferred; and as we disapproved of his model, we thought it imprudent to give him an opportunity of moulding our treaty by it. Whether the minister was influenced by what he really thought best for us, or by what he really thought would be best for France, is a question which, however easy or difficult to decide, is not very important to the point under consideration. Whatever his motives may have been, certain it is that they were such as opposed our system; and as in private life it is deemed imprudent to admit opponents to full confidence, especially respecting the very matters in competition, so in public affairs the like caution seems equally proper.

Secondly. . . . Had we communicated the articles, when ready for signing, to the French Minister, he doubtless would have complimented us on the terms of them; but, at the same time, he would have insisted on our postponing the signature until the articles then preparing between France, Spain, and Britain should also be ready for signing—he having often intimated to us that we should all sign at the same time and place.

This would have exposed us to a disagreeable dilemma. Had we agreed to postpone signing the articles, the British Cabinet might, and probably would, have taken advantage of it. They might, if better prospects had offered, have insisted that the articles were still *res infectae*—that Mr. Oswald had exceeded the limits of his instructions —and, for both these reasons, that they conceived themselves still at liberty to depart from his opinions, and to forbid his executing, as their commissioner, a set of articles which they could not approve of . . . .

Our withholding . . . the knowledge of these articles until after they were signed was no violation of our treaty with France, and therefore she has no room for complaint, on that principle, against the United States . . . .

But Congress positively instructed us to do nothing without the advice and consent of the French Minister, and we have departed from that line of conduct. This is also true; but then I apprehend that Congress marked out that line of conduct for their own sake, and not for the sake of France. The object of that instruction was the supposed interest of America, and not of France; and we were directed to ask the advice of the French Minister because it was thought advantageous to our country that we should receive and be governed by it.

Congress only, therefore, have a right to complain of our departure
from the line of that instruction.[70]

Despite Livingston's distress, the reactions were favorable. Jefferson
wrote to Jay in April, 1783, sending his ". . . homage for the good work
you have completed for us, and congratulating you on the singular happiness of having borne so distinguished a part both in the earliest and
latest transactions of this revolution. The terms obtained are in deed great,
and are so deemed by your country."[71]

Hamilton, who had been critical of the commissioners to Congress,
wrote to Jay in July, 1783.

I have been witness with pleasure to every event which has a tendency to
advance you in the esteem of your country; and I may assure you with sincerity,
that it is as high as you could possibly wish. All have united in the warmest
approbation of your conduct. I cannot forbear telling you this, because my
situation has given me access to the truth, and I gratify my friendship for you
in communicating what cannot fail to gratify your sensibility.

The peace which exceeds in the goodness of its terms, the expectations of the
most sanguine does the highest honor to those who made it. It is the more agreeable, as the time was come, when thinking men began to be seriously alarmed
at the internal embarrassments and exhausted state of this country. The New
England people talk of making you an annual *fish-offering* as an acknowledge-
ment of your exertions for the participation of the fisheries.[72]

On Jay's role, John Adams wrote years later, "A man and his office were
never better united than Mr. Jay and the commissioner for peace. Had he
been detained in Madrid, as I was in Holland, and all left to Franklin . . .
all would have been lost."[73]

After months of discussion, the British finally notified the American
commissioners that with an appropriate preamble and minor changes the
preliminary articles were to be signed as the definitive treaty, and the
final amenities were completed at Versailles on September 3, 1783.[74]

[70] Jay, *Correspondence and Papers*, III, 56–61. July 19, 1783.
[71] Thomas Jefferson, *The Papers of Thomas Jefferson*. ed. Julian P. Boyd (Princeton: Princeton University Press, 1950——. 17+ vols.), VI, 261. April 11, 1783.
[72] Alexander Hamilton, *The Papers of Alexander Hamilton*, ed. Jacob E. Cooke and Harold C. Syrett (New York: Columbia University Press, 1961——. 9+ vols.), III, 416.
[73] John Adams, *The Works of John Adams*, ed. Charles Francis Adams (Boston: Little, Brown and Co., 1850–1856. 10 vols.), IX, 516.
[74] The final treaty left out the secret article in the preliminary treaty that established a boundary between the United States and West Florida if the English regained their control of that area during the war; as they did not the secret article was unnecessary. The provisions of the final treaty are in Morris, *op. cit.,* pp. 461–465.

JAY'S PLEA FOR JUSTICE FOR THE TORIES

In the months prior to and after the signing of the definitive articles, Jay spent much of his time writing letters to his friends back home. Through these letters one can sense the continuing development of his strong sense of nationalism. His experiences in Europe had conditioned him to distrust the motives of other nations. Unless America was strong enough internally she might have great difficulty in maintaining her independence against the external intrigues which must constantly threaten her. To Jay the key to this strength was national spirit and stability administered by a government with enough power to govern in fact as well as name, yet never at the expense of liberty and justice. Thus the question of the fate of the Tories was a vital one. The treaty called for full restitution of their rights by individual states, yet there was clear indication that these rights would be ignored, and reports of assaults on Loyalists circulated in Europe. Robert Livingston wrote to Jay that these reports were exaggerated.

. . . your friends in Europe will find their apprehensions ill-founded, and that the race of tories will not, after all be totally extinct in America. Perhaps, by good training and by crossing the breed frequently (as they are very tame), they maybe rendered useful animals in a few generations.[75]

Still Jay was concerned that the attitude of Americans might reflect that of Governor Clinton who said he would "rather roast in hell to all eternity than . . . show mercy to a damned Tory."[76] In letters to his father-in-law, William Livingston, and to Alexander Hamilton Jay made his views on justice for the Tories quite clear. To Livingston he wrote in July, 1783:

I am happy to hear that the provisional articles meet with general approbation. The tories will doubtless cause some difficulty, but that they have always done, and as this will probably be the last time, we must make the best of it. A universal indiscriminate condemnation and expulsion of those people would not redound to our honour, because so harsh a measure would partake more of vengeance than of justice. For my part, I wish that all except the *faithless and the cruel* May be forgiven. That exception would indeed extend to very few; but even

---

[75] Jay, *Correspondence and Papers,* III, 98.

[76] Allan Nevins, *The American States during and after the Revolution 1775–1789* (New York: The Macmillan Co., 1924), p. 269.

if it applied to the case of one only, that one ought, in my opinion, to be saved.

The reluctance with which the States in general pay the necessary taxes is much to be regretted; it injures both their reputation and interest abroad, as well as at home, and tends to cherish the hopes and speculations of those who wish we may become and remain an unimportant, divided people. The rising power of America is a serious object of apprehension to more than one nation, and every event that may retard it will be agreeable to them. A continental, national spirit should therefore pervade our country, and Congress should be enabled, by a grant of the necessary powers, to regulate the commerce and general concerns of the confederacy; and we should remember that to be constantly prepared for war is the only way to have peace.[77]

On the same theme, Jay wrote to Hamilton in September:

The American newspapers, for some months past, contain advices that do us harm. Violences, and associations against the tories, pay an ill compliment to government, and impeach our good faith in the opinions of some, and our magnanimity in the opinions of many. Our reputation also suffers from the apparent reluctance of taxes, and the ease with which we incur debts without providing for their payment. The complaints of the army—the jealousies respecting Congress—the circumstances which induced their leaving Philadelphia—and the too little appearance of a national spirit, pervading, uniting, and invigorating the confederacy, are considered as omens which portend diminution of our respectability, power, and felicity. I hope that, as the wheel turns round, other and better indications will soon appear. I am persuaded that America possesses too much wisdom and virtue to permit her brilliant prospects to fade away for the want of either. But, whatever time may produce, certain it is that our reputation and our affairs suffer from present appearances.

The tories are as much pitied in these countries as they are execrated in ours. An undue degree of severity towards them would, therefore, be impolitic as well as unjustifiable. They who incline to involve that whole class of men in indiscriminate punishment and ruin, certainly carry the matter too far. It would be an instance of unnecessary rigour,

---

[77] Jay, *Correspondence and Papers*, III, 54–55.

and unmanly revenge, without a parallel, except in the annals of religious rage, in times of bigotry and blindness. What does it signify where nine tenths of these people are buried? I would rather see the sweat of their brows fertilizing our fields than those of our neighbours, in which it would certainly water those seeds of hatred which, if so cultivated, may produce a hedge of thorns against us. Shall all be pardoned then? By no means. Banish and confiscate the estates of such of them as have been either faithless or cruel, and forgive the rest.

Victory and peace should, in my opinion, be followed by clemency, moderation, and benevolence, and we should be careful not to sully the glory of the revolution by licentiousness and cruelty. These are my sentiments, and however unpopular they may be, I have not the least desire to conceal or disguise them.[78]

Return to the United States

As Livingston had resigned as Secretary for Foreign Affairs on June 4, 1783, and Congress had not yet filled the post, official communications to the commissioners was virtually at a standstill. Their original instructions did not allow them to negotiate commercial treaties with England and other countries, and they were patiently waiting for Congress to send a new commission. Jay seemed content to leave this matter to Adams and Franklin and made ready to return to America in the spring of 1784. In May, once accounts of his Spanish mission were in order, he and his wife sailed for home, unaware that Congress had named him to the vacant post on foreign affairs.[79]

[78] *Ibid.*, pp. 90–91. September 28, 1783.
[79] On the same day they elected Jay, Congress appointed Jefferson to join Adams and Franklin for the purpose of negotiating commercial treaties with the powers of Europe (Jay, *Correspondence and Papers*, III, 126).

95

CHAPTER VI

A Secretary for Foreign Affairs

When Jay arrived in New York on July 24, 1784, he was informed of his election as Secretary for Foreign Affairs; official word was sent by Charles Thomson, Secretary of Congress, who declared: "I do not know how you will be pleased with the appointment, but this I am sure of—that your country stands in need of your abilities in that office."[1] Jay had not sought this office and was not anxious to accept it. When it seemed that Congress might appoint him as minister to either France or England, he had declined, and now he seemed content to return to his law practice and family life. However, his state once again elected him to Congress, and he was urged by his friends to accept the appointment as Secretary. LaFayette wrote:

Until a few days ago, I had no doubt but to hear that you had accepted the appointment conferred upon you. My fears, however, have been raised, and with my usual frankness I assure you that your refusal could not but be attended with very bad circumstances. . . . I hope you will accept; I know you must.[2]

Despite such entreaties, it was not until Congress decided to sit in New York, rather than the less accessible Trenton, New Jersey, and agreed to the condition that he be allowed to appoint his own clerks, that Jay finally accepted the appointment.[3] He took the oath of office in late December, 1784. Meanwhile the city of New York, wishing to recognize the contributions of Jay during the war, awarded him a gold box with the following address:

[1] John Jay, *Correspondence and Public Papers of John Jay*, ed. Henry P. Johnson (New York: G. P. Putnam's Sons, 1890–1893. 4 vols.), III, 126.

[2] William Jay, *Life of John Jay* (New York: 1958. J. & J. Harper, 1833. 2 vols.), II, 158–159.

[3] *The American Secretaries of State and Their Diplomacy*, ed. Samuel Flagg Bemis (New York: Pageant Book Co., 1958. 10 vols.), I, 200.

The revolution, which hath secured our liberties and independence, will not be more celebrated for the illustrious events which have marked its progress, than for the role of statesmen and heroes by whose wisdom and valour, under the Divine favour, it has been established on the most solid basis.

Among these worthy patriots you, sir, are highly distinguished. In our own convention, in our first seat of justice, as a member and as president of the United States in Congress assembled, and as a minister plenipotentiary both in Spain and France—you have executed the important trusts committed to you with wisdom, firmness, and integrity, and have acquired universal applause.

While you thus possess the national confidence and esteem for a series of eminent services, we your fellow-citizens, feel a singular pleasure in embracing this opportunity to present you with the freedom of your native city, as a public testimony of the respectful sentiments we entertain towards you, and as a pledge of our affection, and of our sincere wishes for your happiness.[4]

In his new post Jay assumed that the Secretary should conduct the business of foreign affairs, and insisted that correspondence in this area be directed through him prior to being received and examined by Congress. In a letter of January, 1785, he said: "I have some reason . . . to apprehend that I have come into the office of Secretary for foreign affairs with Ideas of its Duties, and Rights somewhat different from those which seem to be entertained by Congress."[5]

In February Congress accepted Jay's interpretation of the duties of the Secretary and declared:

all communications to as well as from the United States in Congress assembled on the subject of foreign affairs, be made through the Secretary for the department of foreign affairs; and that all letters, memorials or other papers on the subject of foreign affairs, for the United States in Congress assembled, be addressed to him.[6]

The Secretary was not a member of Congress, but had the privilege of appearing before that body to express his views, and Jay did so on several occasions. With the authority to determine what issues on foreign affairs should be transmitted to Congress and to appear before Congress to argue

---

[4] Jay, *Correspondence and Papers*, III, 126–127. Monaghan points out that Johnson has misdated the time of the presentation. It was not in July, when Jay returned, but in October, after the Common Council had voted in September to make such awards, not only to Jay but also to Washington, Governor Clinton, LaFayette, and Von Steuben. Frank Monaghan, *John Jay: Defender of Liberty* (New York: The Bobbs-Merrill Co., 1935.)

[5] Cited in *The American Secretaries of State*, I, 201.

[6] *Ibid.*

his views, the new Secretary was an influential figure in the national government.

During his term of office he was perhaps the most prominent man left at home at the national level: Adams was Minister to England, Jefferson to France; Franklin returned to state politics as President of the Pennsylvania Executive Council; Patrick Henry became Governor of Virginia; John Hancock, elected President of Congress in 1785, refused to come to New York and was serving as Governor of Massachusetts; Gouverneur Morris was practicing law in Philadelphia; Hamilton was doing the same in New York; Washington was in retirement at Mount Vernon.

DIVIDED RESPONSIBILITY

The Articles of Confederation, officially agreed to by Congress in November of 1777, but technically not ratified and in force until March, 1781, created the confederacy that provided the basis for government during and after the Revolutionary War. Article II of that document, however, stated that "each state retains its sovereignty, freedom and independence," and each state seemed determined to maintain its autonomy, quite obviously at the expense of central authority. Jay had seen the lack of national spirit and power threaten to disrupt negotiations time and again; while he was still in France in September, 1783, and he had written to Gouverneur Morris that "no time is to be lost in raising a national spirit in America. *Power to govern the confederacy, as to all general purposes should be granted and exercised* . . . every thing conducive to union and constitutional energy of government should be cultivated cherished and protected."[7] Now, as Secretary for Foreign Affairs, directly representing Congress in its relations with other nations, Jay was to find that establishing independence was more difficult than winning it—unless the United States became really united and sufficient power was created to allow it to function with adequate central authority. His reports to Congress and his letters, especially these to Adams, Jefferson, and Washington, reflect his great concern with the situation and his hope that a stronger federal structure would be created.

RELATIONS WITH ENGLAND

Our relations with England were complicated by the fact that the English government had rejected the policy of building a close and cordial understanding with the newly independent United States allowing her all the benefits of reciprocity in commercial trade in an effort to build a political solidarity in their mutual interest; instead the English government

[7] Jay, *Correspondence and Papers*, III, 85.

decided to treat the United States as a rival nation, hoping to undo the results of an unsuccessful war and a humiliating peace.[8] The British steadfastly refused to negotiate a commercial treaty with the new nation, restricting American commerce wherever possible, secure in the knowledge that American merchants had no choice but to continue to do business with merchants in England. Also, under pressure from Canadian fur traders, the English refused to evacuate their posts in what was now the northwestern United States—in a clear violation of the peace treaty. They later justified with some logic their continued presence in that area on the grounds that America was violating the treaty in its failure to protect Loyalists and to honor their claims, but it is clear that the decision to remain in these posts was made prior to the ratification of the treaty itself.[9]

[READING NO. 32]

JAY'S CRITICISM OF BRITISH POLICY

Jay was perplexed by this policy; he regarded the English position as illogical. In September, 1785, he wrote to Adams in London:

It is manifestly as much their [the British] interest to be well with us as it is ours to be well with them; and yet the gratification of resentments, occasioned by disappointment, seems to take the lead of more elevated and useful principles of action.

They expect much from the trade of America, and yet they take pains to cut off every source within their reach by which we may make remittances. It is strange that they should wish us to buy, and yet be so industrious to put it out of our power to pay. Such a system must cause loss of money to their merchants and loss of reputation to ours. I wish most sincerely that credit was at an end, and that we could purchase nothing abroad but for ready money. Our exportations would then be equally profitable, and as our importations would be diminished, we should have less to pay. Domestic manufactures would then be more encouraged, and frugality and economy become more prevalent. . . .

Certain however it is, that mutual civility and respect must, in the

---

[8] British reaction to the peace settlement is discussed in detail in *The American Secretaries of State*, I, 209–226.

[9] On the day before George III proclaimed the ratification of the treaty, the Governor-General of Canada was sent word not to withdraw the garrisons from their frontier posts on the grounds that the treaty, in saying "all convenient speed," did not fix a definite time (*ibid.*, p. 227).

nature of things, precede mutual benevolence and kindness. The manner of your reception and treatment indicated their attention to this consideration, and yet the detention of the posts, the strengthening their garrisons in our neighbourhood, the encouragement said to be given to settlers in those parts, and various other circumstances speak a language very different from that of kindness and good will.

They may hold the posts, but they will hold them as pledges of enmity; and the time must and will come when the seeds of discontent, resentment, and hatred, which such measures always sow, will produce very bitter fruit.

I am well informed that some of the loyalists advise and warmly press the detention of the posts. It is strange that men, who for ten years have done nothing but deceive, should still retain any credit. I speak of them collectively; among them there are men of merit: but to my knowledge some of the most violent, the most bitter and implacable, and yet most in credit, are men who endeavoured to play between both parties, and vibrated from side to side as the appearance of success attracted them. Nay, the accounts of losses which many of them have presented afford conclusive evidence of their inattention to truth and common decency. Such, however, has been the infatuation of British counsels, that what was manifest to others was problematical, if not entirely dark, to them.[10]

[READING NO. 33]
AN UNPOPULAR POSITION ON BRITISH CLAIMS

When Adams protested the failure to evacuate the posts, the British reminded him that America had failed to adhere to the Loyalist claims, and he transmitted this information to Jay, who, at the request of Congress, made a lengthy study of the matter.[11] It was obvious that many Americans resented any favorable treatment of the Tories. While many Loyalists sensed the deep animosity against them and fled the country, others returned to their former homes seeking to re-establish their rights; violence broke out in several states, and virtually every state refused to comply with the

[10] Jay, *Correspondence and Papers*, III, 165–166.

[11] *The American Secretaries of State*, I, 229.

provisions of the treaty.[12] While still preparing his report, Jay wrote to Washington in June, 1786, that the evidence clearly indicated that America had not adhered to her obligations.

It is true that the treaty has been violated. On such occasions I think it better fairly to confess and correct errors, than attempt to deceive ourselves and others by fallacious, though plausible, palliations and excuses. To oppose popular prejudices, to censure the proceedings and expose the improprieties of States, is an unpleasant task, but it must be done. Our affairs seem to lead to some crisis, some revolution, something that I can not forsee or conjecture—I am uneasy and apprehensive; more so than during the war. Then we had a fixed object, and though the means and times of obtaining it were often problematical, yet I did firmly believe we should ultimately succeed, because I was convinced that justice was with us. The case is not altered; we are going and doing wrong, and therefore I look forward to evil and calamities.[13]

Jay's lengthy report on the posts was presented to Congress in secret session in October, 1786. He left no doubt that while violations existed on both sides, the states were in error in failing to execute the terms of the treaty. He summarized his findings in a letter to Adams in November:

The result of my inquiries into the conduct of the States relative to the treaty, is, that there has not been a single day since it took effect on which it has not been violated in America, by one or other of the States; and this observation is just, whether the treaty be supposed to have taken effect either at the date of the exchange of the provisional articles, or on the day of the date of the definite treaty, or of the ratification of it.[14]

On the basis of Jay's report, Congress recommended that the states comply with the provisions, but when they failed to do so, Congress had

---

[12] New York's passage of a confiscation act in October, 1779, set up a procedure for not only the banishment of fifty-nine named Loyalists—who could be put to death without benefit of clergy if they were found in the state—but also confiscated their estates. When it authorized the sale of the land in May, 1784, and instituted fresh confiscatory measures, New York was in clear violation of the treaty. Harry Yoshpe, *Disposition of Loyalist Estates in the Southern District of New York* (New York: Columbia University Press, 1939), p. 114.

[13] Jay, *Correspondence and Papers, III*, 203–204.

[14] *Ibid.*, p. 214.

no power to coerce them. The relations between the two nations were at a standstill: the British would not relinquish the posts until America accepted its responsibility to the Loyalists, and the states, bitter over Tory activities during the Revolution, refused to go along. Adams remained in London until 1788, when he resigned as Minister, but no further progress on the posts was made while Jay was Secretary for Foreign Affairs; with Congress powerless to control commerce, possessing no capacity for tariff reprisal or trade prohibition, it was impossible to negotiate a commercial treaty.

Relations with Spain

The Spanish sent Don Diego de Gardoqui, who had known Jay during his days on the Spanish mission, to negotiate a treaty with the United States that recognized Spain's claim to exclusive control of the Mississippi River below the southern boundary of the United States. Gardoqui, recognizing a streak of vanity in Jay, regarded him as "a very self centered man, which passion his wife augments."[15] He felt that by catering to Jay and his wife and other members of Congress, the influence of Spain might be subtly increased. Although Gardoqui entertained lavishly, there is no evidence that the envoy's plan was effective.

Jay did conclude, however, in the course of the negotiations, that since Gardoqui would not yield on the Mississippi, and in order to obtain favorable trade concessions, the United States should agree to give up the right to navigate the river below the southern boundary for thirty years, at the same time being careful not to concede the principle of American right to it.[16] Jay sought permission from Congress to amend his original instructions to permit him to negotiate on the basis of his recommendation, reminding Congress that in Spain he had opposed our giving up our *right* to the Mississippi and had not changed his mind, but since America had no pressing reason to navigate the Mississippi for many years and could not force it without a possible war with Spain for which we were unprepared, "Why, therefore, should we not (for a valuable consideration, too) consent to forbear to use what we know is not in our power to use."[17]

Jay, however, had broached the matter to James Monroe of Virginia before presenting it to Congress, and Monroe, seeing Jay's proposal as a threat to the welfare of the southern states, united them in opposition to a change in the Secretary's instructions.[18] The seven northern states accepted

[15] Cited in *The American Secretaries of State*, I, 240–241.
[16] *Ibid.*, pp. 243–244.
[17] Cited in Monaghan, *op. cit.*, p. 259.
[18] *The American Secretaries of State*, I, 244.

Jay's recommendation, but since it was a bare majority and, under the Articles of Confederation, a treaty had to be ratified by a two-thirds vote, it was clear that Congress would never accept a treaty forbearing the use of the Mississippi below our southern boundary.

Monroe's letter to Patrick Henry in August, 1786, reveals his suspicions of Jay's role in this matter.

This is one of the most extraordinary transactions I have ever known, a minister negotiating expressly for the purpose of defeating the object of his instructions, and by a long train of intrigue & management seducing the representatives of the states to concur in it.[19]

Monroe's private feelings seem hardly justified. His fellow Virginian, George Washington, agreed with Jay on the wisdom of this policy.[20] Two years later, when Jay's role on the Mississippi question was explosively introduced into the Virginia Convention, which was considering the ratification of the Constitution, another Virginian, James Madison, regarded it, perhaps more sensibly, as matter of judgment.

With respect to the secretary of foreign affairs, I am intimately connected with him. I shall say nothing of his abilities and attachment to his country. His character is established in both respects. He has given a train of reasoning which governed him in his project. If he was mistaken, his integrity and probity, more than compensate for the error.[21]

[READING NO. 34]

JAY'S DEMAND FOR ACTION ON THE MISSISSIPPI QUESTION

Jay and Gardoqui continued to negotiate the Mississippi question, but some northern states joined their southern brothers in opposition to relinquishing navigation rights, and Jay wisely refrained from forcing the matter before Congress. The Spanish continued to control the river and even arrested American citizens who ventured into the disputed area, making the situation more difficult. Finally, in April, 1787, Jay requested that Congress give him express instructions on the Spanish negotiations, but they delayed action until after the constitutional convention had completed their deliberations in September, and then called only for another

---

[19] James Monroe, *The Writings of James Monroe,* ed., Stanislaus M. Hamilton (New York: G. P. Putnam's Sons, 1898–1903. 7 vols.), I, 148.

[20] *The American Secretaries of State,* I, 248.

[21] James Madison, *The Writings of James Madison,* ed. Gaillard Hunt (New York: G. P. Putnam's Sons, 1900–1910. 9 vols.), V, 182.

report by the Secretary.[22] Now Jay put it clearly before Congress. He recommended that we should declare to Spain our right to navigate the Mississippi in a firm and decided manner but

in case of refusal, it will be proper for the United States then to declare war against Spain, there being no respectable middle way between peace and war, it will be expedient without delay for one or the other: for circumstances which call for decision seem daily to accumulate . . . . If Congress conceive that a treaty with Spain on the terms proposed (i.e., forbearance to use the navigation for a term of years) is eligible, the sooner these ideas are communicated to your Secretary the better. If an idea of obtaining better terms should be entertained, the sooner that question can be decided the better; and for that purpose your Secretary thinks it would be well either to place some other negotiator in his stead, or to associate one or more persons with him in the business . . . . He takes the liberty of bserving, that a treaty disagreeable to one half of the nation had better not be made, for it would be violated; and that a war disliked by the other half, would promise but little success, especially under a government so greatly affected by popular opinion.[23]

But Congress did not squarely face its dilemma. It did not agree to forbear, to protest, or to prepare for war, but instead decided that the free navigation of the Mississippi was a clear and essential right of the United States and resolved:

that no further progress be made in the negotiations with Spain by the Secretary for Foreign Affairs; but that the subject to which they relate be referred to the federal government which is to assemble next March.[24]

Jay was no longer responsible, but the problem was not resolved, only temporarily shelved, to rise again while Washington was President. The decision of Congress to postpone action, however, proved a wise one. In 1795 Pinckney's Treaty gave the United States the right of navigation on the Mississippi "in its whole breadth from its source to the ocean." It opened the door to western expansion, permitting the natural growth of the United States without war with Spain. Jay had realized that America could ill

[22] *The American Secretaries of State,* I, 248.
[23] Cited in *ibid.,* pp. 248–249.
[24] *Ibid.,* p. 250.

afford a major conflict, but had not recognized the immediate importance of the western lands. It was an error in judgment, but, as Madison pointed out, an honest one.

Relations with France

While Vergennes and later his successor, Montmorin, were not enthusiastic over Jay's appointment as Secretary for Foreign Affairs—the memory of the latter's role in the peace settlement was still vivid—the relations between France and the United States remained cordial. The French established free ports in the West Indies, which opened them to American ships. While there was hope on both sides to build a profitable trade, the main purpose for such concessions on the part of France seems to have been political—to draw the United States further away from England, who steadfastly refused to negotiate a commercial treaty.

[READING NO. 35]
JAY'S ADVICE AGAINST A CONSULAR AGREEMENT

The treaty of commerce of 1778 between the United States and France had stipulated that each nation had the right to have in the other's ports consuls and lesser officials whose functions were to be worked out by mutual agreement; Congress sent the plan of such a consular agreement to Franklin, and one was signed by Franklin and Vergennes in 1782, but Jay, as Secretary, discovered that Congress had never ratified it and that Franklin had made concessions that had not been authorized. The most serious deviation provided that consuls might appoint agents with consular privileges and immunities to serve throughout the country, creating a system of surveillance that, to Jay, had ominous potential if misused.[25] He carefully delineated for Congress the discrepancies between their original draft and Franklin's agreement and made a strong case against ratification, but out of deference to French sensibilities he did not recommend outright rejection. He reported to Congress:

Although the true policy of America does not require, but on the contrary, militates against such conventions; and although your Secretary is of opinion that the convention as it now stands, ought not to be ratified, yet as Congress have proceeded so far in the present instance,

[25] Jay's role in the consular matter is discussed in detail from a strongly positive viewpoint by Bemis *(ibid.,* pp. 253–259). An examination of Jay's motives that is more critical is in Julian Boyd, "Two Diplomats between Revolutions, John Jay and Thomas Jefferson," in *Virginia Magazine of History,* LXVI (April, 1958), 131–146.

he thinks that instructions should be sent to their Minister at Versailles, to state their objections to the present form, and to assure the King of the readiness of Congress to ratify a convention made agreeable to the scheme before mentioned, provided an article be added to limit its duration to eight or ten years, in order that practice and experience may enable them to judge more accurately of its merits than can ever be done on mere theoretical establishments, however apparently expedient.[26]

Congress accepted Jay's advice, and through Jefferson, a new agreement, which granted consular privileges only to consuls and their immediate aides, but restricted their power, was signed in 1788; it became the first treaty to receive the formal ratification of the United States Senate in 1789.[27] It gave the new nation more breathing room, setting an important precedent in consular conventions. Jay's caution and persistence had paid off.

[READING NO. 36]

DEBT AS A MATTER OF HONOR

The United States owed France more than six million dollars at the end of the Revolutionary War. Interest payments on that part of the loan—made by Dutch bankers, but underwritten by the French government—were barely met, and then when payments on the principal became due in 1785, Congress could raise no money, and bankruptcy ensued. France made little effort to press her claims, however the French government did let the United States know that the debt was still alive.[28] To the Secretary for Foreign Affairs there was no middle ground on this matter. He wrote to Jefferson in July, 1786:

To be respectable abroad, it is necessary to be so at Home, and that will not be the Case until our public Faith acquires more confidence, and our government more Strength . . . . I am happy . . . that . . . France . . . will probably continue disposed to wish us well and do us good, especially if we honestly fulfil our pecuniary Engagements with her. These Engagements, however, give me much Concern. Every principle and consideration of Honor, Justice and Interest calls upon us for good Faith and Punctuality, and yet we are unhappily so circum-

[26] Cited in *The American Secretaries of State,* I, 257.
[27] The terms of this treaty are detailed in *ibid.,* pp. 257–259.
[28] *Ibid.,* p. 259.

stanced that the Monies necessary for the Purpose are not provided, nor in such a Way of being provided as they ought to be. This is owing not to any Thing wrong in Congress, but to their not possessing the Power of Coercion without which no Government can possibly attain the most salutary and constitutional Objects. Excuses and Palliations, and Applications for more Time, made bad Remittances; and will afford no Inducements to our Allies or others to afford us similar Aids on future Occasions.[29]

Relations with the Barbary Pirates

The plight of the new government was agonizingly apparent in our relations with the Barbary States—Algiers, Morocco, Tripoli, and Tunis—states on the Mediterranean coast of Africa that for years had been carrying out piratical operations against the ships of all nations who refused to pay them tribute. American ships were seized and their crews held captive until ransom money was paid. When Jay received a report that Algiers had declared war against the United States, he felt that a war might give the government the unity and strength it needed to survive. He suggested that possibility to John Adams in Ocober, 1785.

[READING NO. 37]
JAY'S VIEWS ON BRIBING THE BARBARY PIRATES

The Algerines, it seems, have declared war against us. If we act properly, I shall not be very sorry for it. In my opinion it may lay the foundation for a navy, and tend to draw us more closely into a federal system. On that ground only we want strength and could our people be brought to see it in that light, and act accordingly, we should have little reason to apprehend danger from any quarter.[30]

Both Adams and Jefferson, however, felt that the United States should undertake negotiations with the Barbary States, borrowing whatever money was needed to purchase peace wherever they could find it; they wrote Jay a joint letter to that effect.[31]

[29] Thomas Jefferson, *The Papers of Thomas Jefferson*, ed. Julian P. Boyd (Princeton: Princeton University Press, 1950———. 17+ vols.), X, 135–136. July 14, 1786.

[30] Jay, *Correspondence and Papers*, III, 173. October 14, 1785.

[31] *Ibid.*, p. 196.

Jay's report to Congress in May, 1786, recommended that no new loan be undertaken, accepted the idea of negotiating treaties, but insisted that the proposal to borrow money be transmitted to the states. At the same time he probed at fundamental weaknesses in the structure of the government:

As to authorizing and instructing them [Adams and Jefferson] to endeavour to borrow money for the purpose in Europe, your Secretary much doubts the policy of it.

The probability of their borrowing so much money appears questionable.

Because those nations to whom our war with the Barbary States is not disagreeable will be little inclined to lend us money to put an end to it.

Because no funds are yet provided for paying even the interest of our former loans, either foreign or domestic.

Because the payments due France, though pressed, have not been completed.

Because the reluctance of the States to pay taxes, or to comply with the economical requisitions of Congress, or to give efficacy to their Federal Government, are topics of common conversation in Europe.

If a loan should be attempted and not succeed, the credit and respectability of the United States would be diminished by the attempt.

Your Secretary thinks that neither individuals nor States should borrow money without the highest probability at least of being able punctually to repay it; and that States should never attempt a loan without having previously formed and arranged adequate funds for its discharge.

It appears to your Secretary improper to open such a loan, even if the success of it were certain.

Because, as the Federal Government, in its present state, is rather paternal and persuasive than coercive and efficient, Congress can make no certain dependence on the States for any specific sums to be required and paid at any given periods, and consequently are not in a capacity safely to pledge their honour and their faith for the repayment of any specific sums they may borrow at any given period, which must be the case if they should make this or any other loan.

Because, as the people or generality will never provide for the public expenses, unless when moved thereto by constitutional coercion, or by the dictates of reason, or by their feelings; and as the first of these motives is here out of the question, your Secretary thinks it probable that the States, on being applied to, will be more disposed to supply money to purchase these treaties of peace while they feel the evils resulting from the war, than they will to supply money to repay borrowed sums when all their fears and dangers from . . . Algerine corsairs, and the pirates of Tunis and Tripoli are vanished and gone.

For these reasons your Secretary is much inclined to think that a fair and accurate state of the matter should be transmitted to the States, that they should be informed that the sum of [no amount stated] will be necessary to purchase treaties from the Barbary States, and that until such time as they furnish Congress with their respective portions of that sum, the depredations of those barbarians will, in all probability, continue and increase.[32]

However, states did not act to furnish Congress with the necessary funds, and in December, 1786, Jay concluded, in a letter to Jefferson, that despite the humanitarian needs of the American captives, the government was powerless to relieve an intolerable situation.[33] Only years later did Jefferson's efforts result in ransoming of American prisoners.

The Weakness of the Confederation

Jay's role in foreign affairs made it increasingly clear to him that the national government must have sufficient power to function decisively. While in Spain he was continually haunted by the financial difficulties of Congress; in France peace negotiations were successfully completed largely because the commissioners assumed more power than their vacillating government was willing to give them. Now as Secretary for Foreign Affairs, his daily activities in attempting to establish normal relations with other nations were continually hampered by government paralysis. It is quite clear from his reports and letters that he was one of the most determined advocates in the country of a much stronger and more stable government than was created in the Articles of Confederation.

The new government's financial difficulties continued to increase. In 1780 Congress had requested from the states the right to levy a duty or impost of one per cent on all exports and imports to provide money to carry on the war, but unanimous consent was needed and neither Rhode

[32] *Ibid.,* pp. 198–199.
[33] *Ibid.,* pp. 222–223.

Island or Georgia would go along. By 1783 Congress proposed, as part of its general revenue plan, an impost of five per cent to last for twenty-five years, which would be effective only when it was accepted by all the states, but which could be done away with by a simple majority vote.[34]

Earlier, when its territory had been occupied by British troops, New York, had strongly supported the idea of increasing the power of the central government, including the power to levy an impost. Governor Clinton wrote to Congress in 1782:

I do not hesitate to give assurances that this State will on her Part chearfully consent to vest the Sovereignty of the United States with every power requisite to an effectual Defence against foreign Invasion and for the Preservation of internal Peace and Harmony; and as an Individual, I can not forbear declaring my Sentiments that the Defects in the Powers of Congress are the chief source of present Embarrasm'ts.[35]

By the end of the war New York's fortunes improved, and as time elapsed, her power and influence continued to increase until she was exercising all but national sovereignty. No longer were Clinton and his followers enthusiastic for the national impost, and when New York levied such a tax of her own—which supplied the state treasury with more than half its revenue from 1784 to 1787—they feared a loss of power and influence for themselves and their state and rejected the national proposal. Many merchants representing the southern part of the state were not satisfied. It was difficult to establish credit and impossible to compete with their British counterparts who had access to the lucrative British West India trade. They published a memorial beseeching the legislature to pass the national impost and to recommend that Congress regulate commerce.[36] But the Clintonians were too deeply entrenched; they refused to accept the recommendation, leaving New York as the only one of the thirteen states who had not agreed to the national tax. Despite the continued efforts of Hamilton and others in New York City, New York's steady refusal doomed the proposal, and perhaps gave the confederation a death blow. Had the power been granted, the confederation would have taken a giant step toward stabilizing its finances; paying interest on foreign and domestic debt would have given the stable interests a firm stake in the government, possibly pumping in enough life for it to survive.

---

[34] Thomas Cochran, *New York in the Confederation* (Philadelphia: University of Pennsylvania Press, 1932). The impost is discussed in detail pp. 133–182.

[35] Cited in *ibid.,* p. 137.

[36] *The Memorial History of the City of New York,* ed. James G. Wilson (New York: New York History Co., 1892–1896. 5 vols.), III, 34.

Still Congress had no power to regulate commerce, and the states continued to become embroiled in disputes with one another over the levying of duties and retaliatory measures. Some of the states, having no convenient ports for foreign commerce, were subject to taxation by their neighbors through whose ports their commerce was carried on. Madison wrote, "New Jersey, placed between Philadelphia and New York was likened to a cask tapped at both ends; and North Carolina, between Virginia and South Carolina, to a patient bleeding at both arms."[37]

In some states the problem of paper money had become acute. The Rhode Island legislature passed a bill making failure to accept the relatively worthless currency of that state a punishable offense. When the supreme court of the state in the case of *Trevett* vs. *Weeden* held that the law was out of harmony with the Rhode Island constitution, the judges were brought up on charges before the legislature. In Massachusetts the debt-ridden farmers of the interior of the state demanded liberal issues of paper money, but instead the legislature, influenced by the more prosperous coastal inhabitants, added to their financial burden by levying extra taxes to pay off the state war debt. The farmers then used the same methods they had used earlier against the hated English "Intolerable Acts"; mobs kept the county courts from sitting, thus preventing the issuance of judgments for debts. When the state militia was called out in September, 1787, Daniel Shay, an officer who had served with distinction during the Revolution, organized more than a thousand men to prevent the district court at Springfield from sitting, because they suspected that the court would indict the leaders of the discontented debtors for treason. Shay's Rebellion, as it was called, was eventually put down by the militia; the fact that the leaders were not executed, but pardoned or let off with short prison terms, and that attempts were made to modify the debt restrictions helped ease the tension and prevented any further eruption in that state. To many Americans who viewed stability and order as vital to the nation's survival, the events in Massachusetts symbolized the confusion and apprehension that seemed to exist everywhere and were final proof that a stronger central authority was necessary.

---

[37] James Madison, *Journal of the Constitutional Convention*, ed. F. H. Scott (Chicago: Scott, Foresman and Co., 1893), p. 33.

[READING NO. 38]
JAY'S POSITION AS A FEDERALIST

Jay had long been concerned with the defects of the confederation. As early as 1785 he had revealed his advanced federalist position.[38] In a letter to his friend James Lowell he declared that the central government should be invigorated as much as possible.

It is my first Wish to see the United States assume and merit the character of one Great Nation, whose Territory is divided into different States merely for more convenient Government and the more easy and prompt Administration of Justice—just as our several States are divided into Counties and Townships for the like purposes. Until this be done the Chain which holds us together will be too feeble to bear much opposition or Exertion, and we shall be daily mortifyed by seeing Links of it giving Way and calling for Repair one after another.[39]

Later the same year he wrote to John Adams:

Your letters, I am sure are useful. They disseminate and enforce those federal ideas which cannot be too forcibly inculcated, or too strongly impressed. Our federal government is incompetent to its objects; and as it is in the interest of our own country, so it is the duty of her leading characters to co-operate in measures for enlarging and invigorating it.[40]

Shay's Rebellion alarmed Jay, who felt that such lawlessness was threatening the cause of liberty itself. In late 1786 he wrote to Jefferson:

[38] In the following pages the term *federalist* will denote a viewpoint that favors a stronger central government and the term *anti-federalist* will represent that which opposes the federalist position for whatever reason. It is not quite fair to infer that the anti-federalists represented a body of opinion that was opposed to greater central authority — for in fact the responsible leaders in that camp were actually for it, but they had seen the development of state constitutions that had created strong legislatures within the independent states and a central government that was subservient to these states, and they felt it necessary to preserve this structure. More power could be given to the central authority, but only through amending the Articles of Confederation, not by changing its basic character; on the other hand the federalists clearly wanted to greatly increase national power and remove the central government from the control of the state legislatures. In the lexicon of historian Merrill Jensen, the anti-federalists can be described as federalists and the federalists are really nationalists. Merrill Jensen, *The New Nation: A History of the United States during the Confederation, 1781–1789* (New York: Alfred A. Knopf, 1950), pp. 422–428.

[39] Iselin MSS., quoted in Monaghan, *op. cit.*, 282.

[40] Jay, *Correspondence and Papers*, III, 172. October 14, 1785.

The inefficacy of our Government becomes daily more and more apparent. Our Credit and our Treasury are in a sad Situation, and it is probable that either the Wisdom or the Passions of the people will produce Changes. A Spirit of Licentiousness has infected Massachusetts, which appears more formidable than some at first apprehended; where similar Symptoms will soon mark a like Disease in several other States is very problematical. . . .

A Reluctance to Taxes, an Impatience of Government, a Rage for Property, and little Regard to the Means of acquiring it, together with a Desire of Equality in all Things, seem to activate the Mass of those who are uneasy in their Circumstances; to these may be added the Influence of ambitious Adventurers, and the Speculations of the many Characters who prefer private to public good . . . . As the Knaves and Fools of this World are forever in Alliance, it is easy to perceive how much Vigour and Wisdom a Government from its Construction and Administration should possess, in Order to repress the Evils which naturally flow from such copious Sources of Injustice and Evil.

Much I think is to be feared from the Sentiments which such a State of Things is calculated to infuse into the Minds of the rational and well intentioned. In their Eyes the Charms of Liberty will daily fade, and in seeking for Peace and Security, they will too naturally turn toward Systems in direct Opposition to those which oppress and disquiet them.

If Faction should long bear down Law and Government, Tyranny may raise its Head, or the more sober part of the people may even think of a King . . . . Changes are Necessary, but what they ought to be, what they will be, and how and when to be produced are arduous Questions. I feel for the Cause of Liberty and for the Honor of my Countrymen who have so nobly asserted it, and who at present so abuse its Blessings. If it should not take Root in this Soil little Pains will be taken to cultivate it in any other.[41]

---

[41] Jefferson, *Papers,* X, 488–489. October 27, 1786.

CHAPTER VII

A Founder of a Federal Union

In the spring of 1785, a joint commission from Maryland and Virginia met at Alexandria, Virginia, to discuss the interstate conflict over the use of Chesapeake Bay and the Potomac River. George Washington invited the delegates to Mount Vernon, where the two states reached agreement on the matters at issue. Maryland suggested holding another conference to discuss commercial questions with the neighboring states, and the Virginia legislature issued a call for such a convention to meet at Annapolis, Maryland, in September, 1786, inviting each state to attend.

[READING NO. 39]
JAY'S REFLECTIONS ON THE ARTICLES OF CONFEDERATION

Jay supported the idea but felt that much more drastic action was needed. In March, 1786, he wrote to Washington:

Experience has pointed out our errors in our national government which call for correction, and which threaten to blast the fruit we expected from our tree of liberty. The convention proposed by Virginia may do some good, and would perhaps do more if it comprehended more objects. An opinion begins to prevail that a general Convention for revising the Articles of Confederation would be expedient. Whether the people are yet ripe for such a measure, or whether the system proposed to be attained by it is only to be expected from calamity and commotion, is difficult to ascertain. I think we are in a delicate situation . . . .[1]

---

[1] John Jay, *Correspondence and Public Papers of John Jay,* ed. Henry P. Johnson (New York: G. P. Putnam's Sons, 1890–1893. 4 vols.), III, 186. March 16, 1786.

Washington, who had strong rapport with Jay on matters of government, responded that it was "necessary to revise and amend the articles of con- federation . . . something must be done or the fabrick must fall; it is cer- tainly tottering."[2]

To Jefferson in August, 1786, Jay spelled out his views on the proper construction of government:

I have long thought and become daily more convinced that the Con- struction of our federal Government is fundamentally wrong. To vest legislative, judicial and executive Powers in one and the same Body of Men . . . can never be wise. In my Opinion those three great Depart- ments of Sovereignty should be for ever separated, and so distributed as to serve as Checks on each other.[3]

Four months later he wrote to Jefferson that he was more convinced than ever that the structure of the government was a major reason for its ineptitude:

I daily become more and more confirmed in the Opinion, that Govern- ment should be divided into executive, legislative and judicial Depart- ments. Congress is unequal to the first, very fit for the second, and but ill calculated for the third. So much Time is spent in Deliberation, that the Season for action often passes by before they decide on what should be done, nor is there much more Secrecy than Expedition in their Measures.—These inconveniences arise not from personal Dis- qualifications, but from the Nature and Construction of the Govern- ment.[4]

[READING NO. 40]
JAY'S ARGUMENT ON THE SOURCE OF AUTHORITY— THE PEOPLE

The meeting at Annapolis was held, but only five states were represented. Despite the poor representation the sentiment for a stronger government was evident. Hamilton, who had proposed such a convention as early as

---

[2] George Washington, *The Writings of George Washington,* ed. John C. Fitzpatrick (Washington, D.C.: United States Government Printing Office, 1931–1944. 39 vols.), XXVIII, 431.

[3] Thomas Jefferson, *The Papers of Thomas Jefferson,* ed. Julian P. Boyd (Princeton: Princeton University Press, 1950–____. 17+ vols.), X, 488–489. October 27, 1786.

[4] *Ibid.,* p. 598. December 14, 1786.

September, 1780,[5] and who attended as a delegate from New York, was chosen to write the report of the meeting. He pointed out some of the conspicuous defects of the Articles of Confederation and asked all the states to send delegates to Philadelphia in May, 1787, to a new convention "to take into consideration the situation of the United States, to devise such further provisions as shall appear to them necessary to render the constitution of the Federal Government adequate to the exigencies of the union."[6]

Jay was not convinced, however, that the proposed convention would have the specific authorization of the people of the states. In January, 1787, he wrote to Washington:

To me the policy of *such* a convention appears questionable; their authority is to be derived from acts of State legislatures. Are the State Legislatures authorized, either by themselves or others, to alter constitutions? I think not; they who hold commissions can by virtue of them, neither retrench nor extend the powers conveyed by them. Perhaps it is intended that this convention shall not ordain, but only recommend; if so there is danger that recommendations will produce endless discussion and perhaps jealousies and party heats.

Would it not be better for Congress plainly and in strong terms to declare that the present Federal Government is inadequate to the purposes for which it was instituted; that they forbear to point out its particular defects or to ask for an extension of any particular powers, lest improper jealousies should thence arise; but in their opinion it would be expedient for the people of the States without delay to appoint State conventions (in the way they choose their general assemblies), with the sole and express power of appointing deputies to a general convention who, or the majority of whom, should take into consideration the Articles of Confederation and make such alterations, amendments, and additions thereto as to them should appear necessary and proper, and which being by them ordained and published should have the same force and obligation which all or any of the present articles now have?

---

[5] In a long letter to his friend James Duane, Hamilton analyzed the weaknesses of the government and recommended calling a general convention of all states with full authority to remedy the situation. Alexander Hamilton, *The Papers of Alexander Hamilton*, ed. Jacob E. Cooke and Harold C. Syrett (New York: Columbia University Press, 1961–——. 9+ vols.), II, 400–418. September 3, 1780.

[6] *Ibid.*, p. 689. September 14, 1786.

No alterations in the government should, I think, be made nor if attempted will easily take place, unless deducible from the only source of just authority—*the People.*[7]

Although Washington was doubtful that revisions in the federal system would insure stable government, he did reassure Jay, declaring that he was willing "to try what the wisdom of the proposed Convention will suggest."[8]

The Federal Constitution, 1787

In February, 1787, Congress issued a formal call for the proposed convention. The sentiment in New York supported such a move, but the Clintonians were wary of the national overtones. The legislature elected a strong federalist in Hamilton, but reduced his influence by selecting two other delegates with anti-federalist views, Robert Yates and John Lansing, to accompany him to Philadelphia. When Hamilton attempted to add two more members to the delegation, including Jay, who was well known for his strong views on national power, he was rebuffed by the New York Senate.[9]

The New York delegates exercised little influence in the Convention, which sat for nearly four months, from May 25 to September 17, 1787. Yates and Lansing found the group too federalist and left in July; they sent a letter explaining their objections to Governor Clinton. Clearly stating their anti-federalist position, they opposed the decision to forego amending the Articles of Confederation and to write an entirely new constitution; they objected to the creation of a national state as being inconsistent with their own state constitution; they regarded centralized government as unwieldy, unworkable, and possibly tyrannical.[10] Hamilton, who attended the sessions infrequently, was disheartened by the relatively weak document that was being created, and his main efforts were concentrated in a five-hour speech in which he presented a plan of government that could function free of state interference.[11] Hamilton's plan received no support, and he

[7] Jay, *Papers and Correspondence,* III, 228–229. January 7, 1787.

[8] Washington, *Writings,* XXIX, 177.

[9] The situation in New York is discussed in detail in Ernest W. Spaulding, *New York in the Critical Period, 1783–1789* (New York: Columbia University Press, 1932), pp. 183–188. A briefer but still valuable account is in Spaulding's "The Ratification of the Federal Constitution," Alexander C. Flick, ed., *History of the State of New York,* V, 29–63.

[10] Cited in Spaulding, *Critical Period,* p. 189, and in Spaulding, "Ratification," in Flick, *History,* V, 42.

[11] Hamilton's plan is discussed in detail in Carl Van Doren, *The Great Rehearsal* (New York: Viking Press, 1948), pp. 91–94.

showed his lack of enthusiasm for other proposals by spending much time in New York. Yet he returned to Philadelphia as New York's only delegate to sign the final document, and despite his reservations became one of its strongest advocates.

[READING NO. 41]

JAY'S HOPES FOR THE PROPOSED CONSTITUTION

As the Convention decided to keep its deliberations secret, people were not sure what progress was being made, but Jay was hopeful. In July, 1788, he wrote to John Adams:

The public attention is turned to the Convention. Their proceedings are kept secret, and it is uncertain how long they will continue to sit. It is nevertheless probable that the importance and variety of objects that must engage their attention will detain them longer than many expect. It is much to be wished that the result of their deliberations may place the United States in a better situation, for if their measures should either be inadequate or rejected, the duration of the Union will become problematical. For my own part I am convinced that a national government, as strong as may be compatible with liberty is necessary to give us national security and respectability.[12]

In early September, as the Convention was drawing to a close, Jay proved himself quite a prophet in a letter to Jefferson:

The Convention will probably rise next Week, and their Proceedings will probably cause not only much Consideration, but also much Discussion, Debate, and perhaps Heat . . . disinterested Patriots and interested Politicians will sit in Council and in Judgment both within and without Doors. There is nevertheless a Degree of Intelligence and Information in the Mass of our People which affords much Room for Hope that by Degrees our Affairs will assume a more consistent and pleasing Aspect.[13]

---

[12] Jay, *Correspondence and Papers*, III, 248–249.

[13] Jefferson, *Papers*, 105–106. September 8, 1787.

[READING NO. 42]
JAY'S SUPPORT OF THE NEW CONSTITUTION

When the results of the Convention were known, Jay's response was favorable. He wrote to Adams in October, 1787:

The public mind is much occupied by the plan of federal government recommended by the late Convention; many expect much good from its institution and others will oppose its adoption. The majority seems at present to be in favor. For my part, I think it much better than the one we have, and therefore that we shall be gainers by the exchange, especially as there is reason to hope that experience and the good sense of the people will correct what may prove to be inexpedient in it. A compact like this, which is the result of accommodation and compromise, cannot be supposed to be perfectly consonant to the wishes and opinions of any of the parties.[14]

But Jay was in error in his contention that most of the people supported the Constitution. The opposition was slowly growing: Patrick Henry, Richard Henry Lee, and George Mason led the opposition in Virginia; Samuel Adams protested in Massachusetts; and in Jay's home state, Governor Clinton marshalled his strong forces against the acceptance of the new document. As the opposition to the Constitution grew, a fierce pamphlet warfare broke out in New York with contributors calling themselves "Aristides," "Brutus," "Cincinnatus," and "Rough Hewer"—the two principals were Clinton, writing as "Cato" and criticizing the Constitution, and Hamilton, writing as "Caesar" and threatening violence to those who opposed the work of the convention.[15] Those who supported the Constitution, however, realized almost immediately that emotional outbursts alone would not save it; three of them; Hamilton, Jay, and Madison—the latter in New York as a member of Congress from Virginia—came together to write a systematic exposition of their point of view. A series of letters, first signed "A Citizen of New York" and later "Publius" to increase circulation in the other states, began appearing regularly in the New York newspapers, the first one printed in *The Independent Journal*, October 27, 1786.[16] The series, eventually printed by almost every newspaper in the state, was

---

[14] Jay, *Correspondence and Papers*, III, 258.

[15] Spaulding, "Ratification" in Flick, *History*, V, 48.

[16] *The Federalist*, ed. Jacob E. Cooke (Middletown: Wesleyan University Press, 1961), xii.

collected and published in book form as *The Federalist,* and circulated widely throughout America.[17]

Although there is dispute as to the authorship of some of the articles, it is clear that Jay wrote five of the essays.[18] Four of them appeared in early November, 1787: Numbers 2, 3, 4, and 5 stressed the importance of union and national power in reducing the influence of other nations over America: "Let candid men judge then whether the division of American into any given number of independent sovereignties would tend to secure us against the hostilities and improper interference of foreign nations."[19]

[READING NO. 43]

JAY'S SUPPORT OF THE TREATY-MAKING POWERS OF THE SENATE

Jay did not write another essay until Number 64, probably because he was incapacitated by a long siege of illness. He had not been well for many months and was finally disabled by rheumatism in the winter of 1787–1788. When he recovered, he made his last contribution to the series in early March, 1788, a ringing defense of the treaty-making powers of the Senate:

They who wish to commit the power under consideration to a popular assembly, composed of members constantly coming and going in quick succession, seem not to recollect that such a body must necessarily be inadequate to the attainment of those great objects, which require to be steadily contemplated in all their relations and circumstances, and which can only be approached and achieved by measures, which not only talents, but also exact information and often much time are necessary to concert and to execute. It was wise therefore in the convention to provide not only that the power of making treaties should be committed to able and honest men, but also that they should continue in place a sufficient time to become perfectly acquainted with our national concerns, and to form and introduce a system for the management of them. The duration prescribed is such as will give them an opportunity of greatly extending their political informations and or rendering their accumulating experience more and more beneficial to their coun-

---

[17] Spaulding, "Ratification" in Flick, *History* V, 49.

[18] The problems involved in determining authorship of the disputed articles are discussed in *The Federalist* (ed. Cooke), xix-xxx.

[19] *Ibid.* (Number 5), p. 27. [Numbers 2, 3, 4, and 5 are printed in their entirety, pp. 8–27.]

try. Nor has the convention discovered less prudence in providing for the frequent elections of senators in such a way, as to obviate the inconvenience of periodically transferring those great affairs entirely to new men, for by leaving a considerable residue of the old ones in place, uniformity and order, as well as a constant succession of official information, will be preserved.

There are few who will not admit that the affairs of trade and navigation should be regulated by a system cautiously formed and steadily pursued; and that both our treaties and our laws should correspond with, and be made to promote it. It is of much consequence that this correspondence and conformity be carefully maintained, and they who assent to the truth of this position, will see and confess that it is well provided for by making the concurrence of the senate necessary both to treaties and to laws. . . .

Others, though content that treaties should be made in the mode proposed, are averse to their being the *supreme* laws of the land. They insist and profess to believe, that treaties, like acts of assembly, should be repealable at pleasure. This idea seems to be new and peculiar to this country, but new errors as well as new truths often appear. These gentlemen would do well to reflect that a treaty is only another name for a bargain; and that it would be impossible to find a nation who would make any bargain with us, which should be binding on them *absolutely,* but on us only so long and so far as we may think proper to be bound by it. They who make laws may without doubt amend or repeal them, and it will not be disputed that they who make treaties may alter or cancel them; but still let us not forget that treaties are made not by only one of the contracting parties, but by both, and consequently that as the consent of both was essential to their formation at first, so must it ever afterwards be to alter or cancel them. The proposed Constitution therefore has not in the least extended the obligation of treaties. They are just as binding, and just as far beyond the lawful reach of legislative acts now, as they will be at any future period, or under any form of government.

However useful jealousy may be in republics, yet when, like Bile in the natural, it abounds too much in the body politic; the eyes of both become very liable to be deceived by the delusive appearances which that malady casts on surrounding objects. From this cause probably proceed the fears and apprehensions of some, that the President and Senate may make treaties without an equal eye to the interests of all the States. Others suspect that the two-thirds will oppress the remaining third, and ask whether those gentlemen are made sufficiently responsible for their conduct—whether if they act corruptly they can be punished; and if they make disadvantageous treaties, how are we to get rid of those treaties?

As all the States are equally represented in the senate, and by men the most able and the most willing to promote the interests of their constituents, they will all have an equal degree of influence in that body, especially while they continue to be careful in appointing proper persons, and to insist on their punctual attendance. In proportion as the United States assume a national form, and a national character, so will the good of the whole be more and more an object of attention; and the government must be a weak one indeed, if it should forget that the good of the whole can only be promoted by advancing the good of each of the parts or members which compose the whole. It will not be in the power of the president and senate to make any treaties, by which they and their families and estates will not be equally bound and affected with the rest of the community; and having no private interest distinct from that of the nation, they will be under no temptations to neglect the latter.[20]

Although these essays of Publius were scholarly in tone, and therefore not directly affecting many people, they were more widely read than any other tract of their time, and are regarded today as the classic interpretation of the Constitution.[21] Because of the hurried circumstances under which they were written, it is a high tribute to the ability of the three authors that these articles have had such a continuing impact. Madison, in a letter to Jefferson in August, 1788, described the conditions that produced them:

. . . I believe I never have yet mentioned to you that publication [*Federalist*]. It was undertaken last fall by Jay, Hamilton and myself. The proposal came from the two former. The execution was thrown, by the sickness of Jay, mostly on the two others. Though carried on in concert, the writers are not mutually answerable for all the ideas of each other, there being seldom time for even a perusal of the pieces by nay but the writer before they were wanted at the press, and sometimes hardly by the writer himself.[22]

[20] *Ibid.* (Number 64), pp. 433–438.
[21] *Ibid.,* xx.
[22] Madison, *Writings,* V, 246.

[READING NO. 44]
JAY'S ADDRESS TO THE PEOPLE OF NEW YORK, 1788

While Jay was recuperating from his illness, he apparently decided to write his own direct but temperate defense of the Constitution. Called *An Address to the People of the State of New York*, it was published in April, 1788, while Jay was recovering from a head injury incurred in the "Doctor's Riot."[23]

The eighteen-page *Address* contained "striking arguments in favor of adopting the proposed Federal Constitution . . . penned with such moderation of temper and sound judgment, that they cannot fail to make an impression favorable to the Constitution on minds open to conviction."[24]

There are times and seasons, when *general evils* spread general alarm and uneasiness, and yet arise from causes too complicated, and too little understood by many, to produce an unanimity of opinions respecting their remedies. Hence it is, that on such occasions, the conflict of arguments too often excites a conflict of passions, and introduces a degree of discord and animosity, which, by agitating the public mind dispose it to precipitation and extravagance. They who on the ocean have been unexpectedly enveloped with tempests, or suddenly entangled among rocks and shoals, know the value of that serene, self-possession and presence of mind, to which in such cases they owed their preservation; nor will the heroes who have given us victory and peace, hesitate to acknowledge that we are as much indebted for those blessings to the calm prevision, and cool intrepidity which planned and conducted our military measures, as to the glowing animation with which they were executed.

While reason retains her rule, while men are as ready to receive as to give advice, and as willing to be convinced themselves, as to convince others, there are few political evils from which a free and enlightened people cannot deliver themselves. It is unquestionably true,

---

[23] Trouble broke out in New York City when townspeople, objecting to medical students' using cadavers, which they erroneously believed to have come from local graves, threatened bodily harm to a group of young doctors, who had taken refuge in the city jail. When Jay attempted to intervene to disperse the crowd, he was felled by a rock. Only the threatened use of the militia by Governor Clinton prevented real bloodshed (Monaghan, *op. cit.*, p. 291).

[24] *Pamphlets on the Constitution of the United States*, Published during its Discussion by the People, 1787–1788, ed. Paul L. Ford (Brooklyn: Historical Printing Club, 1888), p. 68, quotes Noah Webster, writing in *American Magazine*, April, 1788.

that the great body of the people love their country, and wish it prosperity; and this observation is particularly applicable to the people of a *free* country, for they have more and stronger reasons for loving it than others. It is not therefore to vicious motives that the unhappy divisions which sometimes prevail among them are to be imputed; the people at large always mean well, and although they may on certain occasions be misled by the counsels, or injured by the efforts of the few who expect more advantage from the wreck, than from the preservation of national prosperity, yet the motives of these few, are by no means to be confounded with those of the community in general.

That such seeds of discord and danger have been disseminated and begin to take root in America, as unless eradicated will soon poison our gardens and our fields, is a truth much to be lamented; and the more so, as their growth rapidly increases, while we are wasting the season in honestly but imprudently disputing, not whether they shall be pulled up, but by whom, in what manner, and with what instruments, the work shall be done.

Then the king of Great Britain, misguided by men who did not merit his confidence, asserted the unjust claim of binding us in all cases whatsoever, and prepared to obtain our submission by force, the object which engrossed our attention, however important, was nevertheless plain and simple, "What shall we do?" was the question—the people answered, let us unite our counsels and our arms. They sent Delegates to Congress, and soldiers to the field. Confiding in the probity and wisdom of Congress, they received their recommendations as if they had been laws; and that ready acquiesence in their advice enabled those patriots to save their country. Then there was little leisure or disposition for controversy respecting the expediency of measures—hostile fleets soon filled our ports, and hostile armies spread desolation on our shores. Union was then considered as the most essential of human means and we almost worshiped it with as much fervor, as pagans in distress formerly implored the protection of their tutelar deities. That union was the child of wisdom—heaven blessed it, and it wrought out our political salvation.

That glorious war was succeded by an advantageous peace. When danger disappeared, ease, tranquility, and a sense of security loosened the bands of union; and Congress and soldiers and good faith depreciated with their apparent importance. Recommendations lost their influence, and requisitions were rendered nugatory, not by their want of propriety, but by their want of power. The spirit of private gain expelled the spirit of public good, and men became more intent on the means of enriching and aggrandizing themselves, than of enriching and aggrandizing their country. Hence the war-worn veteran, whose reward for toils and wounds existed in written promises, found Congress without the means, and too many of the States without the disposition, to do him justice. Hard necessity compelled him, and others under similar circumstances, to sell their honest claims on the public for a little bread; and thus unmerited misfortunes and patriotic distresses became articles of speculation and commerce.

These and many other evils, too well known to require enumeration, imperceptibly stole in upon us, and acquired an unhappy influence on our public affairs. But such evils, like the worst of weeds, will naturally spring up in so rich a soil; and a good Government is as necessary to subdue the one, as an attentive gardner or husbandman is to destroy the other—Even the garden of Paradise required to be dressed, and while men continue to be constantly impelled to error and to wrong by innumerable circumstances and temptations, so long will society experience the unceasing necessity of government. . . .[25]

The *Address* was published anonymously, but Sally Jay reported that it "has been received in this State with great approbation; nor has the tribute of applause been withheld from the author, that usually accompanies his writings: for though through modesty his name was concealed, it seems the well-known style discovered him."[26]

While Mrs. Jay's objectivity is certainly open to question, the *Address* did circulate widely, especially in the area around New York, where it ranked with *The Federalist* in the extent of its influence.[27] A contemporary, Samuel Webb, declared in late April, 1788, that "it has had a most astonishing influence in converting anti-federalists to a knowledge and belief that the new Constitution was their only political salvation."[28] Washington, writing from Mount Vernon in May, thanked Jay for sending the *Address*, requesting an extra copy, and declared: "The good sense, forcible observations, temper and moderation with which it is written cannot fail, I should

---

[25] The *Address* in its entirety is found in *ibid.,* pp. 69–86.

[26] William Jay, *Life of John Jay,* (J. & J. Harper, 1833. 2 vols.), I, 263. Monaghan points out that William Jay described the author of this letter as "a friend" rather than his mother (Monaghan, *op. cit.,* p. 293).

[27] Spaulding, "Ratification" in Flick, *History,* V, 49.

[28] *Pamphlets on the Constitution,* p. 68.

think of making a serious impression, even upon the antifederal mind where it is not under the influence of such local views as will yield to no arguments, no proofs."[29]

Franklin, too, approved, but felt that despite the obvious value of the publication that Jay should sign his name to the *Address* to give it additional weight during the critical period when ratification was being considered in New York.[30] In a letter to his friend, John Vaughan, in June, Jay explained his refusal to do so:

I have considered the hint suggested in your letter. My long, I may say habitual, respect for the sentiments of Dr. Franklin, at first inclined me to adopt them relative to the subject in question. Further consideration induced me to suspect that he has estimated the influence of my opinion beyond its value. If the reasoning in the pamphlet you allude to is just, it will have its effect on candid and discerning minds —if weak and inconclusive, my name cannot render it otherwise.[31]

The Poughkeepsie Convention

While most of the other states were calling conventions to consider ratification of the Constitution, New York delayed action. Clinton, a staunch anti-federalist, not sure that a convention would reject the Constitution, apparently hoped that by the tactics of delay enough states would reject the Constitution to make the calling of a New York convention unnecessary. With other states meeting and accepting the Constitution, however, many of his followers could not support indefinite postponement, and in early February, 1788, the legislature issued a call for the election of members to a ratifying convention.

In the election held in April, Jay ran on a ticket in New York City that was pledged to the "establishment of a firm national Government . . . [and] the consolidation of our Union, in which is involved our prosperity, felicity, safety, perhaps our national existence."[32] He was overwhelmingly elected, out-polling all other successful federalist candidates including Hamilton. The overall results of the election appeared a smashing victory for the anti-federalists, however, for Clinton's forces won forty-six out of sixty-five

[29] Washington, *Writings*, XXIX, 499.

[30] Jay, *Correspondence and Papers*, III, 335.

[31] W. Jay, *Life*, I, 263.

[32] *The Memorial History of the City of New York*, ed. James G. Wilson (New York: New York History Co., 1892–1896. 5 vols.), III, 40.

seats.[33] Despite the numerical superiority of the opposition, Jay correctly sensed that the Clintonians were not really unified; he wrote to Washington in May that "the majority of the Convention of this State will be composed of anti-federal characters; but it is doubtful whether the leaders will be able to govern the party."[34]

As the delegates prepared to assemble in Poughkeepsie, the federalists were hopeful. Eight states had already approved the Constitution when New York's convention met; New Hampshire and Virginia had conventions already in session. One more ratification would give life to the new government; however, in neither New Hampshire nor Virginia was ratification a certainty. The New Hampshire convention had met earlier, but finding its members hopelessly divided, had adjourned, and now was meeting again. Virginia, despite Madison's powerful arguments for the Constitution and the additional support of Washington, had a strong opposing faction, led by George Mason, Patrick Henry, and Richard Henry Lee—whose *Letters of the Federal Farmer* was the most widely read of the anti-federalist literature.[35] New York's decision was to be crucial.

Although the federalists were unified in their purpose to obtain immediate and unconditional ratification, and although that in itself gave them a powerful advantage over their opponents, they were wise enough to take an important precaution—to set up a system of rapid communication to link New York with Virginia and New Hampshire. The chief architect was Hamilton, who wrote to Madison in late May that the main hope for ratification in New York was the acceptance of a ninth state previous to her own convention to put added pressure on the Clintonians, therefore Virginia's decision was vital to New York.

It will be of vast importance that an exact communication should be kept between us . . . and the moment *any decisive* question is taken, if favourable, I request you to dispatch an express to me with pointed orders to make all possible diligence, by changing horses, etc. All expenses shall be thankfully and liberally paid.[36]

He wrote to John Sullivan, President both of New Hampshire and of its ratifying convention, in early June:

[33] A county by county breakdown of the vote is detailed in Spaulding, *Critical Period*, pp. 221–231.

[34] Jay, *Correspondence and Papers* III, 334.

[35] Spaulding, "Ratification" in Flick, *History*, V, 49.

[36] Hamilton, *Papers*, IV, 649–650.

permit me to request that the instant you have taken a decisive vote in favor of the Constitution, you send an express to me at Poughkeepsie. Let him take the *shortest route* to that place, change horses on the road, and use all possible diligence. I shall with pleasure defray all expenses, and give a liberal reward to the person.[37]

Hamilton remained in touch with Madison during the critical weeks, and later both New Hampshire and Virginia sent news of ratification to New York, putting an immense pressure on the anti-federalist majority in New York's convention that proved an important factor in the collapse of their cause.[38]

The "instant" communication of the federalists contrasted sharply with that of their opponents. The latter group, although less unified in their purpose, still had such men as Clinton in New York and George Mason in Virginia who attempted to keep in close contact with other anti-federalists; however, there is some evidence that postmasters in some states, federalist in sympathy, openly interfered with the mails, delaying for weeks important anti-federalist letters and pamphlets.[39]

[READING NO. 45]

JAY'S REACTION TO THE OPPOSITION AT POUGHKEEPSIE

When New York met in convention on June 17, 1788, Clinton was elected chairman, giving the anti-federalists an important advantage, but one week later their cause was given a severe setback by the arrival of the news that New Hampshire had become the ninth state to accept the Constitution, making a new government inevitable. Never really unified, they now became more divided than ever. In late June, Jay described the situation to Washington:

The greater number [of anti-federalists] are, I believe, averse to a vote of rejection. Some would be content with recommendatory amendments; others with explanatory ones to settle constructions which they think doubtful; others would not be satisfied with less than absolute and previous amendments; and I am mistaken if there are not a few who prefer separation from the Union to any national government whatsoever. They suggest hints of the importance of this State, of its

---

[37] *Ibid.*, V, 2.
[38] Spaulding, "Ratification," in Flick, *History*, V, 57.
[39] The anti-federalist difficulties with the mails are discussed in Spaulding, *Critical Period*, pp. 256–261, and more briefly in "Ratification" in Flick, *History*, V, 55–56.

capacity to command terms, of the policy of taking its own time, and fixing its own price, etc. They intimate that an adjournment may be expedient, and that it might be best to see the operation of the new government before they receive it. The people, however, are gradually coming right, notwithstanding the singular pains taken to prevent it. The accession of New Hampshire does good and that of Virginia would do more.[40]

One week after the news from New Hampshire, word arrived that Virginia had ratified, rendering a mortal blow to the Clintonians, some of whom had hoped that Virginia and possibly North Carolina, still hesitating, might join New York in their own confederation.[41]

Earlier debates in the convention had followed the same lines, which had been described in newspapers and pamphlets; few men—only six federalists, including Jay, and seven anti-federalists—participated.[42] Hamilton was the dominant figure for the federalists, but he was vigorously opposed by Melancton Smith, strong anti-federalist leader who previously had served New York in the Second Continental Congress and had answered Jay's *An Address to the People of the State of New York* with one of his own.[43] James Kent, a federalist member of the New York convention, claimed that "there was no person to be compared to him in his powers of acute and logical discussion. He was Hamilton's most persevering and formidable antagonist."[44]

After the shattering news from Virginia, even the most die-hard Clintonians knew that ratification was inevitable. It was no longer a question of whether the Constitution was good or not, but whether New York could afford to stay out of the federal union on her own, and whether, if she did, New York City would go along. Rumors had circulated for months that the lower counties of the state, strongly federalist in sympathy, were prepared to secede if the Constitution was rejected. Jay had recognized the possibility earlier when he had written to Washington in May: "an idea has taken air that the southern part of the State will at all events adhere to the Union; and if necessary to that end, seek a separation from the northern."[45] In June Hamilton had written to Madison that the anti-federalists feared that rejection of the Constitution would precipitate a

[40] Jay, *Correspondence and Papers,* III, 346.
[41] Spaulding, "Ratification" in Flick, *History,* V, 55.
[42] Bower Aly, *The Rhetoric of Alexander Hamilton* (New York: Columbia University Press, 1941), p. 106.
[43] *Pamphlets on the Constitution,* pp. 92–115.
[44] Spaulding, "Ratification" in Flick, *History,* V, 53.
[45] Jay, *Correspondence and Papers,* III, 335. May 29, 1788.

crisis that might result in "a separation of the Southern district from the other part of the state."[46]

Even if New York did not split in two, the state, left outside of the union, might easily lose the trade that had kept it financially solvent and be subject to trade discrimination from the neighboring states; New York City would certainly lose the preeminence that it had gained by becoming the seat of Congress.

Now, convinced of the inevitability of ratification of the Constitution, the anti-federalists, in an effort to make acceptance conditional rather than unconditional, released a flood of proposed amendments which were debated for many days.[47] On July 11, Jay moved that the Constitution be ratified "and that whatever amendments may be deemed useful or expedient, ought to be recommended." Four days later Melancton Smith proposed to amend Jay's motion to make any amendments conditional. After several days of heated discussion, the anti-federalist, Samuel Jones, moved that Jay's motion, as amended by Smith, be further amended to be unconditional or to read "in full confidence." In a crucial decision, Smith threw his support to the amendment and it narrowly passed. The battle was really over; the Constitution was assured. A long list of recommended amendments was drawn up and Jay, as chairman of a special committee, helped write a circular letter to the states, advocating a second convention.

[READING NO. 46]

CIRCULAR LETTER FROM THE CONVENTION OF THE STATE OF NEW YORK, TO THE EXECUTIVES OF THE DIFFERENT STATES TO BE LAID BEFORE THEIR RESPECTIVE LEGISLATURES

We, the members of the convention of this State, have deliberately and maturely considered the Constitution proposed for the United States.

Several articles in it appear so exceptionable to a majority of us, that nothing but the fullest confidence of obtaining a revision of them by a general convention, and an invincible reluctance to separating from our sister States, could have prevailed upon a sufficient number to ratify it, without stipulating for previous amendments.

We all write in opinion that such a revision will be necessary to

---

[46] Hamilton, *Papers,* V, 3.

[47] Specific motions and resolutions are recorded in *The Debates and Proceedings of the Constitutional Convention of the State of New York Assembled at Poughkeepsie on the 17th of June, 1788,* A Facsimile Reprint of an Original Copy by Francis Childs, 1788 (Poughkeepsie: Vassar Book Co., 1905). For events noted in this paragraph, see pp. 142–146.

recommend it to the approbation and support of a numerous body of our constituents.

We observe that amendments have been proposed and are anxiously desired by several of the States as well as by this,[48] and we think it of great importance that effectual measures be immediately taken for calling a convention to meet at a period not far remote; for we are convinced that the apprehensions and discontents which those articles occasion cannot be removed or allowed, unless an act to provide for it be among the first that shall be passed by the new Congress.

As it is essential that an application for the purpose should be made to them by two thirds of the States, we earnestly exhort and request the legislature of your State (or Commonwealth) to take the earliest opportunity of making it. We are persuaded that a similar one will be made by our legislature at their next session; and we ardently wish and desire that other States may concur in adopting and promoting the measure.

It cannot be necessary to observe that no government, however constructed, can operate well unless it possesses the confidence and goodwill of the great body of the people; and as we desire nothing more than the amendments proposed by this or other States be submitted to the consideration and decision of a general convention, we flatter ourselves that motives of mutual affection and conciliation will conspire with the obvious dictates of sound policy, to induce even such of the States as may be content with every article in the Constitution to gratify the reasonable desires of that numerous class of American Citizens who are anxious to obtain amendments of some of them.

Our amendments will manifest that none of them originated in local views, as they are such as if acceded to must equally affect every State in the Union.

Our attachment to our sister States, and the confidence we repose in them, cannot be more forcibly demonstrated than by acceding to a government which many of us think imperfect, and devolving the power of determining whether that government shall be rendered perpetual in its present form, or altered agreeable to our wishes or a minority of the States with whom we unite.

[48] The substance of the New York amendments is strikingly similar to that contained in the Bill of Rights, the first ten amendments to the Constitution, ratified by three-fourths of the States December 15, 1791. The New York proposals are discussed in Spaulding, *Critical Period*, p. 264.

We request the favour of your Excellency to lay this letter before the legislature of your State (or Commonwealth) and we are persuaded that your record for our national harmony and good government will induce you to promote a measure which we are unanimous in thinking very conducive to those interesting objects.[49]

The letter was unanimously accepted by the delegates, and the next day, July 26, 1788, the convention ratified the Constitution by the vote of thirty to twenty-seven and adjourned.[50] New York had joined the Union.

Hamilton was acclaimed[51] for the triumph at Poughkeepsie, and rightly so, for without his tireless efforts in keeping the federalists informed and united and his dramatic arguments on expediency that caused the most influential anti-federalist, Melancton Smith, to finally support ratification, victory might not have been possible. Jay's role, although somewhat obscured by the brilliance of Hamilton, nonetheless was an important one; his was the voice of moderation and conciliation that helped to soothe the inflamed passions of both sides.[52] During a particularly heated moment of the Convention, James Kent recorded Jay's comment: "We did not come here to carry points, or gain party triumphs. We ought not to expect it or wish it . . . . The laurels of mere party victory might be . . . stained with the blood of our fellow citizens"[53]; the circular letter, temperate in tone and fair in spirit, reflected his concern for a solution that both sides could support, and its unanimous acceptance insured that the final vote for ratification would be a positive one. His contribution had not gone unnoticed. Washington wrote from Mount Vernon in August: "I now congratulate you on the success of your labours to obtain an unconditional ratification of the proposed Constitution in the Convention of your State."[54]

Many years later, in 1815, John Adams in a letter to his friend James Lloyd assessed Jay's role:

---

[49] Jay, *Correspondence and Papers,* III, 353–355. Although the letter had little effect in the other states—no second convention was ever called—it was vital to the ratification of New York.

[50] *Debates and Proceedings* p. 146.

[51] Even before New York had completed ratification, a grand parade in honor of the ten states that had accepted the Constitution was held in New York City. The center of attraction was a large float labeled "Federal Ship—Hamilton" (*The Memorial History of the City of New York,* III, 43).

[52] While the federalists were celebrating the accession of Virginia in early July, they were interrupted by anti-federalists, and a riot resulted. For several days afterward feelings ran high between the two groups (Aly, *op. cit.,* p. 125).

[53] Cited in *ibid.,* p. 114.

[54] Washington, *Papers,* XXX, 34.

I forbore to mention one of more importance than any of the rest, indeed as much weight as all the rest. I mean Mr. Jay. That gentlemen had as much influence in the preparatory measures in digesting the Constitution, and obtaining its adoption, as any man in the nation.[55]

The New Government

North Carolina did not ratify until November, 1789; Rhode Island, faced with the possibility of being left outside the Union, finally accepted the Constitution in May, 1790. The new government, however, did not wait for the two reluctant states. The Constitution was scheduled to go into effect the first Wednesday in March, 1789, and while many members were delayed in reaching New York (seat of the new government), both houses of Congress were duly organized by the first week in April. The electoral vote revealed that only Washington, named on each of the sixty-nine ballots, and Adams, listed on thirty-four, had more votes than John Jay, who was third with nine. Washington reluctantly agreed to serve, and he was inaugurated in late April, 1789. Two months later he asked Jay to review with him important matters concerning the foreign affairs of the United States.[56]

JAY'S RECOMMENDATIONS FOR A DEPARTMENT OF STATE

The two men conferred throughout the spring and summer of 1789, which resulted in Washington's accepting the details of Jay's plan to reorganize the Office for Foreign Affairs into the Department of State. Passed by Congress and signed by Washington in July and September, 1789, the two bills firmly placed control of foreign affairs in the hands of the President. The Secretary was:

to perform and execute such duties as shall, from time to time be enjoined on or intrusted to him by the president of the United States, agreeable to the constitution, relative to correspondence, commissions, or instructions, to or with public ministers or consuls, from the United States, or to negociations with public ministers from foreign states or princes, or to memorials or other applications from foreign public ministers or other foreigners, or to such other matters respecting for-

[55] John Adams, *The Works of John Adams*, ed. Charles Francis Adams (Boston: Little Brown and Co., 1851–1866. 10 vols.), X, 115.
[56] Washington, *Writings*, XXX, 344. June 8, 1789.

eign affairs as the president of the United States shall assign to the
said department; And furthermore, that said principal officer shall
conduct the business of the said department in such a manner as the
president of the United States shall from time to time, order or
instruct.[57]

It was rumored that Washington had offered Jay his choice of positions
in the new government, and that the latter chose to become Secretary of
the Treasury.[58] Washington, however, while requesting Jay to remain as
acting Secretary of State until Jefferson returned from France, appointed
him to the post of Chief Justice of the Supreme Court, where he served
until 1795. Washington's letter to Jay announcing his appointment both
summarizes the past and portends the future for his good friend from
New York:

In nominating you for the important station, which you now fill, I not
only acted in conformity to my best judgment; but I trust I did a
grateful thing to the good Citizens of these United States; and I have
full confidence that the love which you bear to our Country, and a
desire to promote the general happiness, will not suffer you to hesitate
a moment to bring into action the talents, knowledge and integrity
which are so necessary to be exercised at the head of that department
which must be considered as the key-stone of our political fabric.[59]

Although he longed to retire from public life, Jay could not ignore his
country's call to preside over "the key-stone of our political fabric." He
used his "talents, knowledge and integrity" as chief magistrate for a relatively short time, but — through the later decisions of John Marshall —
his influence continued long after he left the bench. While Jay was still on
the Supreme Court, Washington sent him on a special mission to England,
resulting in a highly controversial but vital treaty that helped the new republic avoid a war that it could ill afford. Jay culminated his political career
as Governor of New York, serving two terms with the same dedication to
principle that had characterized his whole life. When at last he stepped
down from public service, John Jay could reflect on a career that had been
built on his faith in the fundamental dignity of man, one that had led to
the founding of a state and nation.

[57] Cited in The American Secretaries of State, ed. Samuel Flagg Bemis (New York: Alfred
A. Knopf, 1928. 10 vols.), I, 275–276.
[58] Monaghan, op. cit., p. 301.
[59] Washington, Writings, XXX, 428–429. October 5, 1789.

Selected Bibliography

Works by John Jay

JAY, JOHN. *Correspondence and Public Papers of John Jay*. Edited by Henry P. Johnson. New York: G. P. Putnam's Sons, 1890–1893. 4 volumes.

————. *Diary of John Jay during the Peace Negotiations of 1782*. Introduction by Frank Monaghan. New Haven: Yale University Press, 1934.

————. "The Federalist, Numbers 2, 3, 4, 5, and 64," *The Federalist*. Edited by Jacob E. Cooke. Middletown: Wesleyan University Press, 1961.

Works by Jay's Contemporaries

ADAMS, JOHN. *Diary and Autobiography of John Adams*. Edited by L. H. Butterfield. Cambridge: Harvard University Press, 1961. 3 volumes.

————. *The Works of John Adams*. Edited by Charles Francis Adams. Boston: Little, Brown and Co., 1851–1866. 10 volumes.

CLINTON, GEORGE. *The Public Papers of George Clinton*. Edited by Hugh Hastings and J. A. Holden. Albany: The State of New York, 1899–1914. 10 volumes.

FRANKLIN, BENJAMIN. *The Papers of Benjamin Franklin*. Edited by Leonard W. Larabee. New Haven: Yale University Press, 1959–——. 9+ volumes.

————. *The Works of Benjamin Franklin*. Edited by Jared Sparks. Boston: Tappan, Whittemore and Mason, 1840. 10 volumes.

HAMILTON, ALEXANDER. *The Works of Alexander Hamilton*. Edited by Henry Cabot Lodge. New York: G. P. Putnam's Sons, 1904. 12 volumes.

————. *The Papers of Alexander Hamilton*. Edited by Jacob E. Cooke and Harold C. Syrett. New York: Columbia University Press, 1961–——. 9+ volumes.

JEFFERSON, THOMAS. *The Papers of Thomas Jefferson*. Edited by Julian P. Boyd. Princeton: Princeton University Press, 1950–——. 17+ volumes.

————. *The Writings of Thomas Jefferson*. Edited by Paul L. Ford. New York: G. P. Putnam's Sons, 1892–1899. 10 volumes.

MADISON, JAMES. *Journal of the Constitutional Convention.* Edited by
E. H. Scott. Chicago: Scott, Foresman and Co., 1893.
————. *The Writings of James Madison.* Edited by Gaillard Hunt. New
York: G. P. Putnam's Sons, 1900–1910. 9 volumes.
MONROE, JAMES. *The Writings of James Monroe.* Edited by Stanislaus M.
Hamilton. New York: G. P. Putnam's Sons, 1898–1903. 7 volumes.
MORRIS, GOUVERNEUR. *The Diary and Letters of Gouverneur Morris.*
Edited by Anne C. Morris. London: Kegan Paul, Trench and Co., 1899.
2 volumes.
PAINE, THOMAS. *The Selected Work of Tom Paine.* Edited by Howard
Fast. New York: Random House, 1943.
WASHINGTON, GEORGE. *The Writings of George Washington.* Edited by
John C. Fitzpatrick. Washington, D.C.: United States Government
Printing Office, 1931–1944. 39 volumes.

Other Primary Sources

Essays on the Constitution of the United States, Published during its Dis-
cussion by the People, 1787–1788. Edited by Paul L. Ford. Brooklyn:
Historical Printing Club, 1892.
Journals of the Continental Congress 1774–1789. Edited by Worthington C.
Ford and Gaillard Hunt. Washington, D.C.: United States Government
Printing Office, 1904–1937. 34 volumes.
*Journals of the Provincial Congress, Provincial Convention, Committee of
Safety and Council of Safety of the State of New York, 1775–1777.*
Albany: T. Weed, New York State Printer, 1842. 2 volumes.
Letters of Members of the Continental Congress. Edited by Edmund C.
Burnett. Washington, D.C.: The Carnegie Institution of Washington,
1921–1936. 8 volumes.
Pamphlets on the Constitution of the United States, Published during its
Discussion by the People, 1787–1788. Edited by Paul L. Ford. Brooklyn:
Historical Printing Club, 1888.
*The Debates and Proceedings of the Constitutional Convention of the
State of New York Assembled at Poughkeepsie on the 17th of June,
1788,* A Facsimile Reprint of an Original Copy by Frances Childs,
1788. Poughkeepsie: Vassar Book Co., 1905.
*The Debates in the Several State Conventions on the Adoption of the
Federal Constitution.* Edited by Jonathan Elliot. Philadelphia: J. P.
Lippincott and Co., 1861. 5 volumes.
The Federalist. Edited by Jacob E. Cooke. Middletown: Wesleyan Univer-
sity Press, 1961.

The Revolutionary Diplomatic Correspondence of the United States. Edited by Francis Wharton. Washington, D. C.: United States Government Printing Office, 1889. 6 volumes.

Works About Jay

BOYD, JULIAN. "Two Diplomats between Revolutions, John Jay and Thomas Jefferson." *Virginia Magazine of History,* LXVI, April, 1958.
Concise Dictionary of American Biography. Edited by Joseph G. E. Hopkins, *et al.* New York: Charles Scribner's Sons, 1964.
Dictionary of American Biography. Edited by Allen Johnson and Dumas Malone. New York: Charles Scribner's Sons, 1928–1944. 22 volumes.
JAY, WILLIAM. *The Life of John Jay.* New York: J. & J. Harper, 1833. 2 volumes.
MONAGHAN, FRANK. *John Jay: Defender of Liberty.* New York: The Bobbs-Merrill Co., 1935.
 Monaghan had access to the Iselin Collection, which contains valuable Jay material, some of which is still unpublished. This material, through the efforts of Mrs. Arthur Iselin, great-great-granddaughter of John Jay, had been preserved until recently in the vault in John Jay's old homestead at Bedford House in Westchester County and is now at Columbia University in preparation for an up-to-date edition of Jay's works prepared by Professor Richard Morris.
PELLEW, GEORGE. *John Jay.* Boston: Houghton Mifflin Co., 1890.

Secondary Sources

General History

CHANNING, EDWARD. *A History of the United States.* New York: The Macmillan Co., 1926–1927. 6 volumes.
MORISON, SAMUEL ELIOT. *The Oxford History of the American People.* New York: Columbia University Press, 1965.

Special History

History of the State of New York. Edited by Alexander C. Flick. New York: Columbia University Press, 1933–1937. 10 volumes: especially Volume IV, Chapters Two, Three, and Five; Volume V, Chapters One and Two.
The American Secretaries of State and Their Diplomacy. Edited by Samuel Flagg Bemis. New York: Alfred A. Knopf, 1928. 10 volumes. Reprinted New York: Pageant Book Co., 1958. 10 volumes: especially Volume I.
The Memorial History of the City of New York. Edited by James G. Wilson. New York: New York History Co., 1892–1896. 5 volumes: especially Volume III.

Selected Bibliography

MORRIS, RICHARD, editor. *The Era of the American Revolution.* New York: Columbia University Press, 1939.

Monographs

ABBOTT, WILBUR. *New York in the American Revolution.* New York: Charles Scribner's Sons, 1929.

ALY, BOWER. *The Rhetoric of Alexander Hamilton.* New York: Columbia University Press, 1941.

BECKER, CARL. *The History of Political Parties in the Province of New York, 1760–1776.* Madison: University of Wisconsin Press, 1909.

COCHRAN, THOMAS. *New York in the Confederation.* Philadelphia: University of Pennsylvania Press, 1932.

COE, SAMUEL G. *The Mission of William Carmichael to Spain.* Baltimore: Johns Hopkins University Press, 1928.

DANGERFIELD, GEORGE. *Chancellor Robert R. Livingston of New York, 1746–1813.* New York: Harcourt, Brace and World, 1960.

DECKER, MALCOLM. *Brink of Revolution: New York in Crisis, 1765–1776.* New York: Argosy Antiquarian Ltd., 1964.

FARRAND, MAX. *The Framing of the Constitution.* New Haven: Yale University Press, 1913.

FLICK ALEXANDER C. *Loyalism in New York during the American Revolution.* New York: Columbia University Press, 1901.

HACKER, LOUIS. *Alexander Hamilton in the American Tradition.* New York: McGraw–Hill, 1957.

JENSEN, MERRILL. *The New Nation: A History of the United States during the Confederation, 1781–1789.* New York: Alfred A. Knopf, 1950.

MINER, CLARENCE E. *The Ratification of the Federal Constitution by the State of New York.* New York: Columbia University Press, 1921.

MORRIS, RICHARD. *The Peacemakers: The Great Powers and American Independence.* New York: Harper & Row, 1965.

NEVINS, ALLAN. *The American States during and after the American Revolution, 1775–1789.* New York: The Macmillan Co., 1924.

SMITH, PAGE. *John Adams.* Garden City: Doubleday, 1962. 2 volumes.

SPAULDING, ERNEST W. *New York in the Critical Period, 1783–1789.* New York: Columbia University Press, 1932.

VAN DOREN, CARL. *The Great Rehearsal: The Story of the Making and Ratifying of the Constitution of the United States.* New York: The Viking Press, 1948.

YOSHPE, HARRY. *The Disposition of Loyalist Estates in the Southern District of New York.* New York: The Columbia University Press, 1939.

138